These are the WORDS:

*A Vocabulary
of Jewish Spiritual Life*

Arthur Green

כשרות

Kashrut: Fitness

תשובה

Teshuvah: Return

צדיק

Tsaddik: Righteous One

These are the

קדיש

Kaddish: Praise for God

עולם הבא

'Olam Ha-Ba: The World to Come

תיקון עולם

Tikkun 'Olam: Mending the World

הלכה

Halakhah: Walking on the Path

קבלה

Kabbalah: The Received

חבורה

Ḥavurah: Community

שבת

Shabbat: The Sabbath

מדרש

Midrash: Inquiry

תורה

Torah: Teaching

WORDS:

*A Vocabulary
of Jewish Spiritual Life*

Arthur Green

JEWISH LIGHTS PUBLISHING
Woodstock, Vermont

These Are the Words
A Vocabulary of Jewish Spiritual Life

© 1999 by Arthur Green

Library of Congress Cataloging-in-Publication Data
Green, Arthur, 1941–
These are the words : a vocabulary of Jewish spiritual life / by Arthur Green.
p. cm.
ISBN 1-58023-024-5 (hc)
1. Spiritual life—Judaism. 2. Judaism—Terminology. 3. Hebrew language terms
and phrases. I. Title.
BM50.G74   1999
296'.01'4—dc21   99-30221
    CIP

Design and typography by:
    Scott-Martin Kosofsky and Betsy Sarles
    at The Philidor Company, Cambridge, Mass.
    Set in Philidor Fairfield, Philidor Hillel, Philidor Vilna,
    Metro, and Monotype Joanna types.
Illustrations by:
    Joel Moskowitz, from the "Hebrew Blessings" series (pages 1, 37, 73, 113, 147, 191, 233)
    Maty Grünberg (page 211)

First Edition
10 9 8 7 6 5 4 3 2 1
Manufactured in the United States of America
Published by Jewish Lights Publishing
A Division of LongHill Partners, Inc.
Sunset Farm Offices, Route 4
P.O. Box 237
Woodstock, VT 05091
Tel: (802) 457-4000
Fax: (802) 457-4004
www.jewishlights.com

For my sister Paula—
Disciple of Aaron,
Pursuer of Peace.

"Seek peace"—in your own place
"and pursue it"—even to the ends of the earth

Table of Contents
TOPICAL

Table of Contents

ALPHABETICAL

Introduction

Toward a New Jewish Language

"How do you say it in Jewish?" was a frequently asked question in the world of my childhood. It might have been an aunt or a cousin who was posing the question, in the course of trying to explain something to an older relative who had never quite mastered English. Of course, then "Jewish" meant "Yiddish," which is precisely what the word Yiddish means: the language of us *yidn*, the Jews.

Speaking "Jewish" today is a somewhat different matter. Yiddish has lost its place as the *lingua franca* (or *mameloshn*, the "mother-tongue") among Ashkenazic Jews (Jews whose origins are in Central and Eastern Europe), and spoken Hebrew has increasingly become identified as the language of Israelis. A new language of international communication has emerged within the Jewish community. It is called English. Partly because so many of us Jews now live in English-speaking countries and partly because English is the second language of most educated people in the world, including Israelis, it is natural that English has also become the international language of the Jews. This means that we read Jewish books in English, we see Jewish theater in English, we conduct Judaic scholarship in English, we read the Jewish news in English. True, those of us who pray do so, at least partly, in Hebrew and a few of us study classical Hebrew texts. But even these texts we discuss with each other in English, the language we speak for most of our Jewish lives.

There is nothing wrong with English. We happen to have "fallen in" rather well, choosing a linguistic vehicle of tremendous richness and nuance, enriched in an unusually complex way by the many language streams that comprise the Western heritage. The only problem in using English as the new international Jewish language is that it is not *ours* as Jews. The cultural and spiritual heritage that created Jews and Judaism is not the same as that which created the English language. There are important overlaps, to be sure. Both are part of the same Western heritage: In some ways Hebrew Scripture highly influenced English expression and literary tropes. Yiddish and English are related through a common Germanic heritage and some words are similar. But differences remain, and there is reason to be concerned that much of the distinctive flavoring of our heritage is lost if we get it all in English translation.

In the next few generations, a form of Judeo-English is bound to emerge. This will be an English spoken and written by and for Jews that will include elements of Hebrew and Yiddish vocabulary. We thankfully do not live the kind of ghetto existence that would be necessary to produce another Yiddish, which was the product of Jews' severe isolation from others. Nor do I suggest that our highly-educated community will—or should—speak the kind of Brooklyn-identified "Yinglish" popular among the post-immigrant generation ("So come over by me and we'll learn a little . . ."). Rather I am proposing that in the course of speaking good and proper English to one another (if Americans are capable of such a thing, my British friends would add!), we integrate a core of essential Jewish words that are shared and understood throughout our community. These words should constitute the basic vocabulary of our religious/communal identity, lending to the "foreign" tongue that we speak a Jewish authenticity and a rootedness in the many centuries of cultural life that have come before us.

Truth be told, it is hard to live out a serious Judaism in translation. Among the world's religions, Judaism has in common with Islam a deep and loving tie to its sacred language. While there are great Islamic works written in Persian, Urdu, and many other languages, any Muslim knows that Arabic, especially the Arabic of the Qur'an, is essential to the Muslim experience. Judaism is quite similar: The teachings of our tradition are so closely tied to Hebrew texts and their subtle meanings, based on close readings and wordplays possible only in the original, that a Judaism lived in translation will never feel quite like the real thing.

Yet we have to accept the reality that not all Jews, or others interested in getting closer to Judaism, will be *able* to learn Hebrew. Mastering Hebrew, especially with the skill needed to appreciate its many subtleties, takes years. Our rapid-paced world unfortunately does not offer everyone the opportunities for study with which some of us have been blessed.

The Power of Words

A tremendous surge of interest in various Jewish mystical and spiritual traditions has recently occurred. "Turned on" by a great variety of spiritual experiences, Jews lacking in basic religious education are coming home to seek out their own tradition. Non-Jews as well, intrigued by the antiquity and richness of Judaism, have sensed that great wisdom lies hidden in Hebrew tomes that they are not able to read. Several different forms of Jewish meditation have acquired a wide following. In these mystical and esoteric aspects of Judaism, an understanding of the key vocabulary and nuances of language is even more essential. Simply rendering terms into English does very little to help the reader, especially when trying to convey the mystical implications. One has to understand the associations that each word evokes, and this often depends on linguistic puns and subtle interrelationships of words that are not carried over in translation.

Hebrew, like other Semitic languages, is based on a three-letter root system. Most nouns and verbs in the ancient Hebrew vocabulary are derived from these three-letter stems. Terms originating from the same root are thought of as related to each other, even if we would render them into entirely different words in English. This network of root patterns lends to the language an associative richness that translation often loses. A classic example of this pattern is found in the relationship between the words *raḥamim* ("compassion" or "mercy") and *reḥem* ("womb"). Both of these words are derived from the stem ם-ח-ר/*r-ḥ-m*. How do you convey to the English reader that God's "mercy" for all creatures is like that of a mother who has carried them in the womb? Or how do we indicate in English that *halakhah* ("Jewish law") is derived from ה-ל-ך/*h-l-kh*, the root for "walking," because it provides the path that we who walk through life are to follow?

These Are the Words is an attempt to create a vocabulary list for people who want a deeper understanding of Jewish life, with an emphasis on the spiritual side. While compiling this book, I have asked myself: "What are the most essential terms that an educated Jewish seeker needs to know? What is the basic vocabulary of the Jewish spiritual life?" For each term, I have offered a definition, some history, and a bit of etymology. Then I have tried to ask what is significant, interesting, or untranslatable about this Hebrew term. Why, in other words, is it *important* for you to know and use this word in Hebrew?

I began this book with a list of 100 words. Since each Jew is traditionally supposed to recite a hundred blessings each day, I thought, let's also learn a hundred words. But soon my list outgrew this limitation. I then decided to stick to 120, which is also a good Jewish number. Moses, after all, lived 120 years, and when we want to bless someone with long life, we say: "To a hundred and twenty!" But the list kept growing. Now there are 148. Since every combination of Hebrew letters can be read either as word or number, I looked at 148 and realized that we (because you, as reader, are part of this enterprise) had stumbled onto something important. The number 148 in Hebrew is written קמח and is pronounced "kemah." Read as a word, however, קמח/*kemah* means "flour." This immediately calls to mind the rabbis' saying "If there is no flour, there is no Torah." Now most commentators read that as a way of saying that even scholars need to be fed (and therefore please give to our scholarship fund . . .). But here we understand "flour" as the raw material needed to bake bread. This book gives you the flour—the linguistic raw material—to "bake" your own Jewish life. You have to mix it with the living water that only you can bring (and hopefully a few eggs . . .) to bake the bread of Torah. (Oops! Due to a late addition, there are now actually 149 entries in this book.)

As you will hopefully discover here, Judaism itself is a language, a group's way of expressing our beliefs, longings, aspirations, dreams. It is these that we want to teach and share with others, then pass on to our children. The vocabulary of Jewish life is the framework through which we hand on the past. It also provides the pegs on which we hang our hopes and dreams for the future.

I therefore invite you to come learn this language with me. Read what I have to say about a given term. Think about it in your own way. Compare my interpretation with others you have been taught by rabbis or teachers, that you've read in other books, or that you've developed on your own. Feel free to take issue with my (often neo-Hasidic) understanding of the tradition or some of my own idiosyncratic interpretations of Judaism. This book intentionally has lots of blank space, some of it in or adjacent to each entry. I urge you to *write* in this book. Use the blank space to add your own interpretations. Make this book your own by sharing in its writing. Have your own comments alongside mine to re-read in later years. Pass on this list, hopefully in your own enriched version, to your next generation.

Torah is a process that never ends. The very fact that each of us stands as a link between those who preceded us and those who will come after us means that we are all transmitters of Torah. To do that work faithfully, we have to learn, absorb, and understand the teachings of all the generations that came before us. Learning the vocabulary of Jewish life is a small but crucial first step in that direction. But a second step comes after that. We have to make the tradition our own, put it into our language, and enrich it with our own concerns. The Judaism we seek to share with others and pass on to our children should be *better* and *richer* because our generation lived it. No tradition can survive merely as an antiquarian legacy, a burdensome past we cannot escape. Only by adding the experience and the example of our own Jewish lives to the legacy we've inherited do we truly hand on a *torat ḥayyim,* a living teaching, to those who come after us.

In dedicating this book to my sister Paula, I have in mind also the countless women like her who were not offered a Jewish education, while we, their brothers, were. Fortunately that situation has changed in our day, but there are still many women (and not a few men) who suffer from having received inadequate Jewish education or none at all. Here, Paula—and all you others—is the basic Judaism you missed, filtered through my years of living with our shared tradition. Enjoy!

Language Notes

Transliteration

This book uses a simplified version of standard scholarly transliteration. The letters of the Hebrew alphabet are rendered according to the following scheme:

א	' (only when occuring in the middle of the word)	ל	L
ב	B, V	מ	M
ג	G	נ	N
ד	D	ס	S
ה	H	ע	' (occuring anywhere in the word)
ו	V	פ	P, F
ז	Z	צ	TS
ח	Ḥ	ק	K
ט	T	ר	R
י	Y	שׁ	SH, S
כ	K, KH	ת	T

Hebrew letters containing the *dagesh ḥazak* (a doubling, which is indicated in Hebrew by a point within the letter) are doubled in English, such as in *kabbalah* and *shabbat*.

A few concessions have been made to conventional English spellings, such as *matzah* and *Hanukkah*.

Singular and Plural Forms

The plural in Hebrew is usually created by adding either -*im* or -*ot* to a word. Since -*ot* is usually the plural of feminine words, the ending -*ah*, indicating the feminine singular, is dropped before the -*ot*. A few examples:

SINGULAR	PLURAL
etrog	*etrogim*
hasid	*hasidim*
tallit	*tallitot*
yeshivah	*yeshivot*

Pronunciation

Modern Hebrew follows the Sephardic tradition in placing emphasis on the last syllable of each word. Thus one should say Yom Kip-PUR, megil-LAH, Tal-MUD, and so forth. In ordinary American-Jewish speech, however, the Ashkenazic accenting of the syllable before the last (Yom KIP-pur, me-GIL-lah, TAL-mud) is widespread. Both are considered correct, with the former perhaps sounding a bit pedantic to some. Both *aleph* and '*ayin* are sounded as glottal stops among Western speakers of Hebrew. Some distinguish between *ḥet,* a light aspirant thickening of the "h" sound, and *khaf,* which is more fully guttural, though that distinction is also lacking in many Western speakers. Vowel sounds are as follows:

a = ah
ai = i as in "fine"
ay = ay as in "day"
e = short e as in "pen"
ey = ay as in "day"
i = short i as in "pin" *or* ee as in "meet"
o = short o as in "son"
u = short oo as in "tool"

A Note on "The Rabbis"

Judaism as we know it was created by the early teachers in what is called the rabbinic period in Jewish history, the age of the *Mishnah** and the *Talmud**, about 100–600 of the Common Era (c.e.). When I speak of "the rabbis" in this book, I refer not to Rabbi Goldberg from the Bronx or Rabbi Shapiro from Chicago, but to the leaders of that formative era.

* An asterisk following any Hebrew term indicates that it is explicated in this volume. See the alphabetical table of contents for the proper page.

אלהות, עולמות עליונים
God and Worlds Above

י–ה–ו–ה
Y-H-W-H

WE BEGIN out of order. All the other words in this book will proceed in English alphabetical order, each within its own category. But this is the word beyond all words, the word that has to come first, the source of cosmic and verbal energy that underlies the existence of all the others.

The *Torah** calls *Y-H-W-H* the name of God. When the Lord appears to Moses at the burning bush to send him on his mission (Exodus 3:15), this name is revealed to him. He is told that this is God's name "forever," though that word is written in a way that also could mean "secret" or "hidden." The commentaries take it to mean that י-ה-ו-ה/*Y-H-W-H* is the hidden, mysterious name of God.

What is its mystery? First, it has no vowels. Without vowels, which usually appear as dots beneath or alongside the letters, it is impossible to pronounce a word. But *Y-H-W-H* also has no real consonants! Y, H, and W really are blowing sounds, rushings of air through the mouth. There is nothing hard or concrete about them, no "B" or "K" sound that requires a definite action of the lips, teeth, or throat. The point is one of *elusiveness* or abstraction. The name of God is so subtle it could slip away from you. *Y-H-W-H* is not a God you can grab hold of and be sure you've got firmly in your mental "grasp."

Y-H-W-H, like most Hebrew words, appears to be derived from a three-letter root. H-W-H is the root for "being" or "existence." The Y at the beginning of *Y-H-W-H* could indicate the imperfect tense, so that we could translate the name to mean "that which is" or "that which will be." But *Y-H-W-H* is more likely to be an awkward conflation of all the tenses, and it is really best to translate it as "Is-Was-Will Be." In fact, the Hebrew word for "being" is HaWaYaH, which is simply a switching around of the letters in Y–H–W–H. The commanding verb of Genesis l, *yehi* or "Let there be," is closely related to it. Y–H–W–H, in fact, is not really a noun at all, but a verb caught in motion, artificially frozen by our simple minds into noun form, a movement conceived as though it were a "thing." This occurs in the same way a still camera might frame an action shot, giving you the impression of having "captured" something motionless.

Not only *can* we not properly pronounce this word; we are not permitted even to try. This "explicit" name of God was to be pronounced only once a year by the high priest in the Holy of Holies on *Yom Kippur**. No lesser setting was considered adequate for its utterance. After the Second Temple was destroyed (in 70 C.E., by the Romans) its pronunciation was forbidden altogether and various other terms, beginning with *adonai**, were substituted for it.

Adonai

Literally "My Lord," a word by which to address one's superior, like "m'lord" in old English usage. Since very early times this term has been used to replace *Y–H–W–H**, which may not be pronounced. When the Hebrew Bible was first translated into Greek (around 200 B.C.E.), it was the word *adonai* that the Greek translators rendered as *kyrios* or Lord.

Midrashic tradition offers an illuminating explanation for the origin of this term as a substitute for the name of God. When God created Adam, it is told, the angels were filled with jealous wrath. "A mere earthling!" they said, denying that Adam had any special worth. But God loved Adam and wanted him to display his wisdom. So God brought forth the animals, one after another, and asked the angels what they were to be called. Having no experience of the animal world, the angels did not know. Then God called Adam and asked him to name the animals. Adam did so in short order. "And now," said God, "what should *you* be called?" Adam answered, "I should be called Adam, for I was taken from *adamah* ('earth')." "And what should I be called?" asked God. "You," Adam replied immediately, "should be called *adonai,* for You are Lord over all Your works."

A twofold lesson can be learned from this *Midrash**. One part is that being Lord over us is not God's most essential Self. The divine essence is better expressed by the name *Y–H–W–H**, for God's presence permeates all of being. It is we humans who ascribe lordship to God, out of *our* need for submission. Lordship is a projection from human society onto the mysterious, unknowable, divine Being. Even though that is true, however, we call God *adonai* even in our most intimate prayers. We use this word as though it really were a name, and those prayers are acceptable. This is the second part of the lesson. Saying "Lord" puts us into *relationship* with Y–H–W–H. This desire for relationship, even with so abstract a being as Y–H–W–H, is a sign of our love. God responds to our love and chooses to be called by this name we made up for God in our infancy, rather than by the Explicit Name itself, Y–H–W–H.

Atah

Tʜᴇ Hᴇʙʀᴇᴡ word for "you" (in the second person masculine singular) may seem like a strange choice for an entry in this spiritual vocabulary list. In modern spoken Hebrew, it is used constantly in conversation without a second thought.

But "you" is also "You"—the pronoun we use when addressing God in prayer. This provides us a good place to reflect a bit on Hebrew, a language in which even the shortest and simplest of words cannot be spoken without profound theological overtones. Because Hebrew was preserved for so long as the language of the synagogue, most Jews for more than 1000 years learned *atah* as the word that followed *barukh* (in the phrase "blessed are You. . .") in the opening to all traditional Jewish blessings.

The philosopher Martin Buber's great insight, in his classic *I and Thou,* is that every "you" we speak contains within it echoes of "the eternal You." This insight came to him because he was thinking in Hebrew. Every *atah*, for the hearer sensitive to Hebrew rhythms, bears within it the *atah* we say when we turn to God in prayer. Every *atah*, then, contains within it some hidden fragment of prayer. Speech is inevitably holy speech, if we look deeply enough into its root. Buber's genius lay in universalizing the Jew's experience of this primal Hebrew word.

The first two letters of *atah* are *aleph* and *tav*. These form the beginning and the end of the Hebrew alphabet. Since the mystical masters believe that God created all the worlds by combinations of letters, *aleph* and *tav* can be seen to stand for all Creation: All that ever was or will be comes about only through the letters from *aleph* through *tav*. (This is something like Jesus' saying, using the Greek alphabet, "I am alpha and omega," meaning "I am the beginning and the end.") But combining those two letters gives us only the word *et,* a particle used for the direct object. *Aleph* to *tav* by themselves refer to the world only as object.

The third letter in *atah*, *heh*, is used here to stand for the name of God. Add God's name to *aleph* and *tav* and the word comes alive. With the *heh* added (even though *heh* is really nothing but a breath!), the word is no longer "it," but "You"! The "aaahh" sound at the end draws us out, connects us to the other. With *atah* we address the living Subject, not the inanimate or abstract object.

Din

DIN is the most common Hebrew term for "judgment." A court is a *bet din* ("a house of judgment"); a judge is a *dayyan*, a person who renders *din*.

One of the best-known depictions of God in Jewish folk tradition is that of the Judge Who presides over the heavenly court. This imagery is especially connected to *Rosh Hashanah**, which is known as *yom ha-din* ("the day of judgment"). Judaism's strong sense of moral accountability calls forth this image. Each of us is responsible for our actions and we are all called before God to account for them.

But the attribute of judgment (*middat ha-din*) is only one side of the Divine Self. God has an equally strong sense of compassion for us since we are all God's children. We thus call upon God to judge us as our Divine Parent, as one Whose love can always be trusted, even when it is punishment that we require.

The precise balancing of these two divine attributes—*din* and *rahamim** ("compassion"), sometimes referred to as the "left" and "right" hands of God—is important in the special symbolism of the *Kabbalah**. There *din*, the judging and punishing side of God, has a fierce and nearly uncontrollable character. When not tempered properly by the force of compassion, it becomes the root of evil, the source within the one God for all that opposes divinity. Evil is thus divine judgment run wild. To put it differently, the Kabbalah teaches that judgment, when not aligned with love and compassion, can be demonic rather than divine.

Dinim, in Kabbalistic language, are negative forces, sparks of evil. They must be restored to God by our acts of worship and "sweetened" as they are returned to their root. These *dinim* should not be confused with *dinim* in halakhic literature, where the word simply means "laws" or "judgments."

Elohim

ELOHIM is the generic Hebrew term for "god." The Bible uses it when referring both to the "God" of Israel and to the "gods" of other nations. The word is also occasionally used in the sense of "great one," referring to a respected human authority.

The most interesting thing about *Elohim* is the fact that it is a plural form. The Bible acknowledges that fact by using it when speaking of "other gods." Then plural verbs or adjectives are used with it, as required by the rules of proper grammar. But when the same plural word is used to refer to the God of Israel, those rules are intentionally violated and *Elohim* is treated as though it were singular. Thus the Bible's opening words, *Bereshit bara' elohim* ("In the beginning God created. . ."), are something of a grammatical abomination! Every time the *Torah** says *va-yomer 'elohim* ("God said") the rules of grammar are broken.

This is, of course, no accident. The point is that *Elohim* in this context is used as a *collective*. All the powers that once belonged to all the deities of the pantheon—such as love, power, wisdom, war, fruitfulness—are now concentrated in this single Being Who contains them all. The blessings needed for every aspect of human life are now all seen to come from a single source. This is the essence of the monotheistic revolution, embodied in the language each time you use this common Hebrew word for "God."

The *Zohar*, the great compendium of *Kabbalah**, opens with a profound interpretation of the word *Elohim*. It reads the word as composed of two shorter Hebrew terms: אלה/*eleh* and מי/*mi*. *Eleh* means "these," referring to all the images and attributes of God available to us through the *sefirot**. *Mi* means "who?" always in the interrogative form. Despite all our thinking and imagining, the *Zohar* teaches, God remains a mystery. If you think you understand God, you lose the "Who?" Then you become an idolater, worshipping your own images, just like those who made the golden calf and said: *"These* are your gods, O Israel!" (Exodus 32:4).

אמת

Emet

TRUTH or *emet* is God's own seal, according to the rabbis. The three letters of the word constitute the first, middle, and last letters of the Hebrew alphabet. Truth has to be broad and open enough to encompass all letters, all words, all of existence. By contrast, שקר/*sheqer* or "lie" consists of three letters huddled together near the end of the alphabet. They make their own closed little circle, and do not allow the light of truth to shine in.

God's seal of truth commands us to be honest and to live with integrity. This has to do with every aspect of our lives, from our business dealings to the way we express our faith in God. What we do and say should be out in the open, accessible to all who want to see it, and capable of passing common human tests of truth.

In the Bible *emet* refers to a deeply held and unshakable belief; it is closely related to the word *emunah** or "faith." The truth of one's position is shown by how firmly it is held. Ultimately that which we are willing to live for and die for becomes our personal truth. It is in this spirit that our liturgy adds the word *emet* to the conclusion of the *shema'**, affirming our personal witness to God's truth.

For the Jewish philosopher, beginning in the Middle Ages, *emet* also means the truth that can be demonstrated by philosophical reasoning. This tradition attributed such truth to Plato and Aristotle, the philosophical giants of ancient Athens, and to the many thinkers, non-Jews as well as Jews, who came in their wake. This meant that there were two sources of truth, the revelation of Sinai and the reasonable conclusions of philosophy. The relationship between these, especially with regard to such difficult questions as

Creation or the nature of prophecy, forms the content of Jewish philosophy.

In modern times, such thinkers as Immanuel Kant and G. W. F. Hegel were given similar status. Much of the German-Jewish philosophical tradition, from Moses Mendelssohn (1729–1786) to Martin Buber (1878–1965), revolved around responses to modern Western philosophies. Again, Jews affirmed in this way that we have no monopoly on truth and that we recognize truth's value no matter from where it comes.

A postmodern Jewish theology emerging in our own day will also have its external "pillars" of truth on which to rest and against which to react. These will probably be derived partly from the new contact of Judaism with Eastern philosophies, especially Buddhism. Jewish-Buddhist dialogue on such topics as the nature of oneness, reality and illusion, and the purpose of human existence may be among the most important sources of truth as Jews pursue it in the coming years.

In dealing with the relationship between Jewish commitment to tradition and the search for truth, we need to constantly reevaluate the meaning of our Jewish religious language and the ways it can continue to evolve. Jewish thinkers since the Middle Ages have understood that Biblical tales and especially depictions of God are to be taken nonliterally. But what is the nature of that nonliteralist faith? Are we to see the language of the prayer book, for example, as myth? Can those mythic images be replaced, particularly if we find them to be in conflict with our truer contemporary beliefs and values? Or does the language have a holiness and canonical status that requires it, like the Bible, ever to be re-interpreted but never changed? Freedom to re-interpret ancient texts is essential to Judaism and provides one of its greatest strengths. But is there a point where re-interpretation flies in the face of intellectual honesty? How do we get by such points and continue to live as thinking and searching Jews?

אֵין סוֹף

Eyn Sof

THIS PHRASE means "no end" or "endless." In its original meaning, it is not a noun or noun phrase; it might be used rather as an adverb to describe an *endlessly* long story or a scene of *endless* beauty. In Kabbalistic (*Kabbalah**) writings of the 12th and 13th centuries, however, it is used to designate the unknowable God. *Eyn Sof* refers to the endless, unaffected, unchanging aspect of existence, that which "was" (although tense is inappropriate to *Eyn Sof*) before the beginning and that which "will be" after the end.

Since it is beyond knowing, *Eyn Sof* may be designated as "transcendent" to the human mind, but that does not mean that it exists "outside" the universe. *Eyn Sof* is no more "beyond" the world than it is "within" all things, for any assertion of boundaries, any assertion of a "two" or an "other" following the one that is *Eyn Sof* would necessarily violate the meaning of this term. It may thus be seen as the "one" of the monistic side of Jewish mysticism, that which knows (but resists admitting!) that *all* is one.

The Kabbalists did distinguish between *Eyn Sof* and the *sefirot**: The ways in which the *sefirot* and ultimately this entire world emerge from within *Eyn Sof* are essential themes of mystical contemplation. So too is the ongoing relationship between the sefirotic universe, depicted in the most colorful imagery, and this endless but indescribable font of being.

Kavod

Kavod or "glory" is the Biblical term for God's presence as manifest in the world. It is especially found in priestly sources, the parts of *Torah** dealing with the *mishkan** ("tabernacle") and the sacrificial system. Sometimes (as in Exodus 24:17) the *kavod* takes on the appearance of a "consuming fire."

Elsewhere, however, *kavod* is a presence that is more intuited than seen. Once the *mishkan* is completed, we are told, Moses cannot enter it "because the cloud had rested upon it and the glory of God filled the tabernacle" (Exodus 40:35). *Kavod* is related to the root כ-ב-ד/k-b-d, which can mean "heavy"; there is a sense of weightiness or filling about the Divine Presence that leaves no room for Moses to enter.

When the prophet Isaiah has his initial vision (Isaiah 6), he hears the angels proclaim of God that "His glory fills all the earth." This is a great universalizing of what had earlier been just a sense of localized Divine Presence in a holy place. Ever since Biblical times, Judaism has sought to maintain both senses of this term in religious experience. The presence of God indeed is everywhere: *Any* place, as the Hasidic masters so well taught, can become a holy Temple and gateway to heaven. But this sense can only be maintained by a tradition that remembers *specific* holy places and records concrete experiences of them.

Kavod tends to be replaced in post-Biblical Judaism by the term *shekhinah** or "indwelling presence."

קליפה

Kelipah

KELIPAH literally means "shell," but idiomatically in Yiddish and in late Hebrew it came to refer to an "evil spirit" or demonic force.

Jewish mystics in the Middle Ages were fascinated by the nut as a symbol of truth. This association was partly based on Song of Songs 6:11: "I have gone down into the nut-garden." The outer shell and membranes of the walnut appear to parallel the cranium and the tissue surrounding the brain. They were seen as protections that kept the unfit away from penetrating the deeper truths of wisdom.

This image of the *kelipah* as protective insulation surrounding the core was transformed by the new Kabbalistic (*Kabbalah**) myth of Rabbi Isaac Luria (1534–1572). Luria claimed that creative energy, in the form of divine light, was sent into this newly-emanated world from the mysterious core of divinity. The light was contained in certain "vessels." The emanated world was not sufficiently holy to contain God's light, however, so the vessels smashed and the sparks of light were scattered. The broken shards of the vessels, which are now called *kelipot,* cover those sparks or keep the divine light hidden. As such, they become active enemies of those who seek the light.

In the popular imagination, the *kelipot* also become tempters, leading humans to do the sorts of evil deeds that will keep the light of God hidden from them. The Ba'al Shem Tov (Rabbi Israel ben Eliezer, 1700–1760, the first *rebbe** of Hasidism) well understood that the *kelipah*'s best weapon in this war is guilt: The more you are filled with and obsessed by your own guilt, the less you are able to see the sparks of divine light that radiate everywhere and throughout all the worlds.

Mal'akh

YES, JUDAISM believes in angels. The Bible is filled with them. Cherubim block the entrance to Eden after Adam is expelled, Isaiah sees seraphim surrounding God in the Temple, and *mal'akhim*, which translates simply as "messengers," appear as the three humble strangers whom Abraham and Sarah fed in their tent.

Angels served as an outlet for compromise or flexibility in the face of ancient Israel's very severe dose of monotheism. What happened to the gods of all the other nations? Were they simply "sticks and stones," as the *Torah** (Deuteronomy 4:28) suggests? What about such cosmic forces, long personified in human imagination, as the god who brings rain or the god who causes the winds to blow? These were allowed to abide in the mythic imagination of Judaism in the form of angels. They are granted no real power of their own, of course; all they can do is God's bidding. Unlike humans, they are ever conscious of their status as divine messengers and they have no evil urge to stray from their Master's service.

Angels play an especially great role in the various Jewish mystical traditions. The divine throne is flanked on one side by Metatron, chief of all the angels who, in an earlier life, was a man named Enoch. On the other side of the throne stands Sandalphon, whose height reaches from earth to heaven. Each day he weaves a new crown for his Creator out of the prayers of Israel. (Miss a prayer one day and you are diminishing the crown of God!)

Most modern Jews live far from this rich fantasy world of archaic religious imagination. Still important, however, is the idea that angels sometimes come disguised in the garb of humans: The angels who visit Abraham are in fact called "men" in the Bible, and it is only tradition that says they were angels. Real human messengers, on the other hand, are sometimes referred to as *mal'akhim,* or "angels." When you meet someone inhabiting a human body, in other words, never pre-judge whether it is a person you are about to encounter or an angel. *That's* the tradition!

Melekh

THE DEPICTION of God as *melekh* or "King" was a key part of the legacy of symbols and images that ancient Israel received from the surrounding cultures. As human kings were revered as gods in the ancient Near East, so too were the gods depicted amid the trappings of royalty.

Post-Biblical Judaism continued to cherish the royal metaphor, perhaps more so than ever once historical circumstance denied the Jews earthly sovereignty. The idea that God is the only true King, and therefore that all flesh-and-blood rulers are more or less usurpers, was widely if quietly believed among Jews for a very long time. An emperor might dare call himself "king of kings," but God remained beyond him, since God was called *melekh malkhey ha-melakhim,* "King over kings of kings"! The liturgy, and especially that of *Rosh Hashanah** and *Yom Kippur*,* is especially enamored of royal imagery.

Depicting God as King did not necessarily make for the remoteness and grandeur generally associated with this image. Rabbinic literature is studded with hundreds of parables comparing God to a human king. Often they show the king struggling with the most normal of human situations: the king having trouble disciplining his son, the king whose dear friend gives him wrong advice, the king whose wife is unfaithful, and so forth. In the course of humanizing God, Jewish texts depicted the Deity in the role of the king who, despite having seemingly unchecked powers, often confronts limiting situations that require acting with restraint, wisdom, and compassion.

Contemporary Jews are often uncomfortable with the royal metaphors they find in so many Jewish sources. These images seem outdated and "irrelevant," hierarchical and repressive. Some Jews have called for such changes as replacing *melekh ha-'olam* ("universal King") in the frequently used blessing formula with *ruaḥ ha-'olam* ("universal Spirit"). Those who argue against such changes note the widespread fascination with royalty still seen in children's fantasies and in products of the creative imagination. To delete kingship from the symbolic repertoire of Judaism might lead to a spiritual impoverishment of the tradition, just the opposite of what is needed in our day. The debate goes on, in this writer's soul as in many others.

Neshamah

NESHAMAH is the usual word for "soul" in Jewish speech. It refers to the essence of the person, the truest self. In Yiddish "*a gute neshomeh*" is "a good-hearted person"; "*a teyere neshomeh*" is "a precious soul," a person of unusual sensitivity or extraordinary devotion.

There is no clear concept of soul (as distinguished from body) in the Bible. The word *neshamah* actually means "breath," the noun form of מ-ש-נ/n-sh-m, "to breathe." It is first used in Genesis 2:7, when God "blew the breath of life (*nishmat ḥayyim*)" into Adam's nostrils. It thus comes to mean "life-force" or "animating spirit" in various Biblical contexts.

In the rabbinic period, partially under Hellenistic influence, Judaism developed a full-fledged notion of soul. Here the *neshamah*, a daily restored gift from "above," is sent by God to dwell in the body, whose origin is worldly. A daily recited prayer asserts the purity of each soul as it was given and acknowledges that God will one day take it back and thus end life. But that same prayer also affirms that the soul will be restored when the dead are resurrected at the end of time. The rabbis believe that each soul is both unique and eternal (*'olam ha-ba**). Between death and resurrection (after a one-year period of purgation, if required by sin) the soul dwells in "the Garden of Eden," where God visits nightly "to take delight in the souls of the righteous."

Neshamah alternates in the early sources with two other terms for soul: *nefesh*, which means "self," and *ruaḥ* or "spirit." Eventually *nefesh, ruaḥ,* and *neshamah* (which are collectively sometimes abbreviated as *NaRaN* in the literature) came to be viewed as three parts or "levels" of the soul. In the Middle Ages, these came to be linked with various neo-Platonic or Aristotelian theories of the tri-partite soul, with *nefesh* as the lowest, followed by *ruaḥ,* and finally *neshamah*.

The Kabbalists (*Kabbalah**) view the soul as an actual "part of God above"; that which God blows into Adam is the presence of God's own Self. Nothing humans can do will eradicate this Divine Presence from the deepest recesses of each person's heart. Some sources try to limit possession of *neshamah* or divine soul to Jews, but this is inconsistent with the belief in universal descent from Adam and Eve and thus contradicts the most essential teachings of Judaism (*tselem elohim**).

The concluding verse of the Psalter (Psalm 150:6) also refers to *neshamah,* and may be translated "May every breath praise God," or "Let each soul praise God. Halleluyah!"

'Olam

Usually translated as "world" or "universe," 'olam has a complex meaning that slides across the space/time continuum. Sometimes the meaning clearly seems to be spatial or geographical. In the *berakhah** formula, *melekh ha-olam* is usually translated "King" or "Ruler of the universe." Elsewhere, however, the term just as clearly refers to time. *Le-'olam*, for example, means "forever" and *me-'olam* usually means "always, since the beginning." In many places, however, the reader is left with a delicious ambiguity. Does the prayer book's *me-'olam ve-'ad 'olam atah el* mean "You have been and will be God forever" or rather "from world to world—even as we travel from one world to another—You are God?" Either reading is quite plausible.

The ancient rabbis spoke of two *'olamot*, this world and the next, or "the world to come," *'olam ha-ba.** In the rather undefined rabbinic talk about future things, *'olam ha-ba* can refer either to our experience of the afterlife or to the perfected world that is "yet to come" in messianic times.

Jewish mystics speak of four *'olamot* or "worlds" that together comprise spiritual reality. These are (in descending order) *atsilut*, the World of Emanation or divinity itself; *beri'ah*, the World of Creation or the object of visionary experience; *yetsirah*, the World of Formation or the realm of the angels; and *'asiyah*, the World of Deed or the realm of human souls. Physical reality, according to most Kabbalists (*Kabbalah**), is outside these four, but sustained by the energies that flow through *'asiyah*. In various Kabbalistic systems, the number of worlds is usually much higher, often reaching into the thousands. This talk of multiple "worlds" in the old Kabbalistic sources has interesting analogues in several contemporary spheres. To the psychologist, multiple "worlds" are an externalization of multiple levels or aspects of consciousness that coexist with one another. To the astrophysicist, however, they represent a part of the varied attempts by pre-moderns to envisage the vastness of space and time, pre-figuring awareness of other solar systems or even other nonphysical dimensions of being.

פרדס

Pardes

PARDES means "orchard" or "garden." It is derived from the ancient Persian word that also gives us "paradise" in English. It came to have religious meaning in Judaism because of a famous tale told in the *Talmud**, perhaps the best-known account of mystical experience preserved in Jewish sources. "Four entered the Pardes," the text begins. "Ben Zoma looked and died, Ben Azzai looked and was damaged [mentally], the other one cut off the plantings, and Rabbi Akiva entered in peace and departed in peace." The "other one," who was Rabbi Elisha ben Abuya, is said to have left the rabbinic path for some sort of heresy. The term *pardes* here seems to represent a symbolic ideal "place" that serves as the inner locus for esoteric speculation. In later Hebrew, those who "stroll in the orchard" are Jews who engage in mystical reflection.

In later times, the four consonants of *PaRDeS* were seen to represent the four accepted levels of Scriptural interpretation. Each verse of the *Torah** could be read for its *Peshat*, or obvious, direct meaning; *Remez*, a "hint" of philosophical or moralizing allegory; *Derash*, the old rabbinic methods of interpretation; and *Sod*, the esoteric or Kabbalistic (*Kabbalah**) meaning. This sense that the text (or any life situation!) simultaneously bears several layers of meaning is characteristic of Jewish thinking. It may have helped to form a characteristically "Jewish" approach to viewing and solving problems, both on an intellectual and a practical level.

רחמים

Raḥamim

"COMPASSION" or "mercy" are the usual translations for *raḥamim*. It is a love and caring for one in need, especially of the sort a parent might have for a wayward but nevertheless needy child.

Raḥamim is etymologically related to *reḥem*, "womb." It is therefore fair to assume that there is something motherly about it, corresponding to the compassion a mother will always have for the child she carried. But in Jewish liturgy it is also associated with the fatherhood of God: "As a father has *raḥamim* for his child, so may You, O Lord, have for us . . ."

The father-God traditionally portrayed by the rabbis is one Who struggles between His own emotional impulses, depicted in impersonal formulations as the aspect of *raḥamim* and the aspect of *din**. *Din* seeks the punishment of humans for their sins, knowing it is for their own good and for society's good as well. *Raḥamim* calls God to compassion and forgiveness, no matter what the cost. God indeed loves the Law, but He needs to be reminded that He loves His frail human creatures even more.

Occasionally *din* is depicted as actual divine anger, and God seeks human help in overcoming His wrath so that He might do what He knows is right, dealing with His children compassionately. In these passages we see reflected the old Biblical legacy of a God (and a human race!) struggling with anger, ready to lash out against sinners unless a Moses-figure can stay anger's hand. This depiction of the deity has been much refined by rabbinic times, but is not entirely absent.

רוח הקדש
Ruaḥ ha-Kodesh

THE "HOLY SPIRIT" or *ruaḥ ha-kodesh* in Judaism is not a specific entity or element within divinity. It rather indicates the presence of God among humans, and is most easily rendered as "inspiration."

Early rabbinic writings do not clearly distinguish between "prophecy" and *ruaḥ ha-kodesh*. They seem to follow the Biblical text itself, where a spirit is present among the prophets that possesses them, sometimes passing from one to another (I Samuel 16:14; II Kings 2:9). The prophet is drawn to follow wherever it leads (Ezekiel 3:14; 11:24). Later Jewish sources, however, place *ruaḥ ha-kodesh* on a lower level than prophecy (*navi**). The *ketuvim* (*hagiographia* or "holy writings"), the third section of the *tanakh**, were written by the inspiration of *ruaḥ ha-kodesh*. This would include David's authorship of the Psalms (*tehillim**) and Solomon's authorship of Proverbs, Ecclesiastes, and the Song of Songs (*Shir ha-Shirim**).

The inspirational presence of *ruaḥ ha-kodesh* continues to abide in the world even after formal prophecy was suspended when the Temple was destroyed. Occasionally the rabbis refer to the presence of the Holy Spirit in their house of study. It is this Spirit that makes for the divine presence in the ongoing halakhic process, which uses legal precedent and human reason to seek out the transrational will of God.

Rare individuals are also said to possess *ruaḥ ha-kodesh*. Sometimes this relates to a claim for clairvoyance and the ability to predict the future; this was the case with the Ba'al Shem Tov (Rabbi Israel ben Eliezer, 1700–1760), his daughter Odel, and several other Hasidic masters. Elsewhere it may be used to describe a person of great piety whose teachings reflect a profundity that can only be accounted for by divine inspiration.

ספירות
Sefirot

THE CENTRAL TALE of *Kabbalah** is an account of how a whole, perfect, and infinitely varied world emerged from within the oneness of God. That oneness is absolute; no "two" may follow the "one" of "one God." Multiplicity therefore arises from *within* that one as successive layers of reality reveal themselves. These rungs, stages, or aspects of God's single Self are called *sefirot*. The tale of how the many emerged from the One is told by the Kabbalists in highly dramatic fashion, using a vast array of symbols. Somewhere in the process there was a flaw, and the divine/cosmic unity has been rent asunder. Now God, the cosmos, and the human soul are in search of a lost harmony. The Kabbalist or mystic is one who can undertake an inward journey that recapitulates this divine process. In the course of this contemplative adventure, he (or she, but that is an entirely new innovation) helps to repair the damage and restore balance to the cosmos as well as to the soul.

The *sefirot* (literally "numbers") are a series of primal emanations, stages in which the divine Self proceeds forth from the absolute hiddenness of *Eyn Sof** and emerges as the complex male-and-female personal God Who, in turn, creates all the lower worlds. These ten stages in the flow of divinity toward the lower world exist both before Creation and throughout history. They are the paths forged by the primal emanation that preceded Creation, but even now they are still the channels of divine energy, active in every moment. Simultaneously these *sefirot* also serve as stages in the mystic's ascent and the rising of the worlds and rungs themselves as they seek re-inclusion within the undifferentiated Godhead. The flow of energy through the sefirotic stages is thus endless and bidirectional.

But seen *functionally* rather than as divine "entities," each of these ten *sefirot* is in effect a group of terms or verbal pictures that the Kabbalists themselves have created. (These are indeed the richest "iconography" of medieval Judaism.) The symbols of the Kabbalists' imagination are organized into ten clusters of word pictures. Each member of a sefirotic cluster is identified with all the others, and when a Kabbalist mentions any one of them, all the others are also called to mind. Thus the Kabbalist might speak of the "right hand" of God, or of silver, milk, morning, south, the myrtle branch, love, or Abraham. One who knows the Kabbalistic system understands that all of these are symbol-terms of the fourth cluster within the *sefirot,* which is usually designated as *ḥesed** or love. In the course of this teaching, especially if it comes (as it often does) in the form of commentary on Biblical or early rabbinic sources, the Kabbalist will switch from one of these symbols to another without missing a beat, reinforcing the cluster of associations in the reader's mind. While talking about the same *sefirah* or pair of *sefirot* in union, the writer may with utmost symbolic grace let his thought flow from water imagery to that of light, from sexual metaphors to those of one or another of the commandments, and then go on to beasts and birds or Jerusalem and the history of the Jews. Significantly, each cluster contains both terms derived from nature (sun and moon, heaven and earth, trees, wells, streams, and oceans) and figures from Jewish tradition. Within a given cluster, all the terms bear the same valence.

Thus the Kabbalists created a *symbolically enriched language.* They felt that they could express a new profundity by using this network of associations that joined nature, Scriptural text, and Jewish religious tradition. This language was seen as the appropriate one for speaking of the inner life of God, a matter too elevated and glorious to be conveyed by ordinary human speech.

For the Kabbalists, the *study* and interpretation of Scripture by Kabbalistic means and the *experience* of the *sefirot* are not separable from one another. Those who speak the special Kabbalistic language do so to simultaneously unlock text and experience. To

ל

speak of the *sefirot* is itself to enter the world of the *sefirot* and to live on that intensified plane of being.

The ten sefirot, along with a few of their many symbolic associations, follow:

1. *Keter*
   Highest Crown. Nothing. The Nothingness of Thought. Intellect.

2. *Ḥokhmah*
   Wisdom. Primal Father. Wine. Primordial Torah. Deep Well. Primal Point. Mind.

3. *Binah*
   Understanding. Mother. Womb. Leah. Repentance. Jubilee. Fiftieth Gate. Spring. Palace. Cranium.

4. *Ḥesed*
   Love. Abraham. South. White. Morning. Silver. Milk. Right Hand.

5. *Din; Gevurah*
   Judgment. Fear. Isaac. North. Red. Dusk. Gold. Blood. Left Hand.

6. *Tif'eret*
   Glory. Jacob. The Blessed Holy One. King Solomon. Man. Truth. East. Bridegroom. Sun. Heaven. Written Torah. Tree of Life. Palm.

7. *Netsah*
   Eternity. Victory. Moses. Cherub. Right Pillar. Source of Prophecy.

8. *Hod*
   Beauty. Praise. Thanksgiving. Aaron. Cherub. Left Pillar. Source of Prophecy.

9. *Yesod*
   Foundation. Joseph. Phallus. Covenant. Staff. Righteous One. Peace. Sabbath Day.

10. *Malkhut; Shekhinah*

Kingdom. Indwelling Presence. Jerusalem. Sabbath Eve. West. King David. Rachel. Woman. Bride. Temple. Tent of Meeting. Moon. Ocean. *Mikveh**. Earth. Vagina. Oral Torah. Tree of Knowledge. Citron.

שׁדּי

Shaddai

Shaddai is the ancient name of God that is often translated "Almighty." The etymology of the term is uncertain. It is often used together with the name *El* in the Bible, and *El Shaddai* may have referred to God as manifest in fields or mountains. The word may be connected to *shad* or "breast." Then *El Shaddai* would refer to a God with breasts, One Who nurses or nourishes the devoted. This meaning is related to the rabbis' assumption that the word is connected to *dai*, "enough," meaning that God offers sufficient sustenance to all in need.

Rabbinic legend connects the etymology of *Shaddai* to a powerful Creation tale. On the second day God created both sea and dry land. The border between them was not clearly fixed, however. The sea, personified as a great watery dragon, kept attacking the land and threatening to swallow it up. God had to step in between them and set the sandy borders of the sea. "Enough!" God shouted, and the sea ceased its expansion. "You set a border they may not cross, lest they return to cover the land" (Psalm 104:9). Here the God called *Shaddai* is the One Who was able to say "Enough!" to the powerful, all-consuming sea.

Today the seas threaten the land once again. Human inventiveness has led us to use and abuse our world in such a way that global temperatures are rising, raising the sea level with them. Many predict great flooding of coastal areas in the years to come. Now it is *we* who have to say "Enough!"

Shekhinah

SHEKHINAH is the indwelling presence of God in this world. It is the divinity we may experience when enthralled by the beauties of nature, in deep encounter with another human being (*neshamah**), or alone in moments of stillness, whenever the heart is open. Judaism claims that this encounter may also take place in the context of sacred study ("Two who are together and study *Torah**, *shekhinah* abides in their midst") and that it also has a moral dimension: *shekhinah* is to be found in human acts of justice and compassion.

Shekhinah is the later term that replaces the Biblical *kavod** or *kevod Y–H–W–H.* It is never seen as a separate deity or "part" of God, Who is One and indivisible. *Shekhinah is* God insofar as God is manifest in this world. *Shekhinah* has a special attachment to the Temple site in Jerusalem. It is said that the Divine Presence, when it wandered into exile with Israel, never fully departed from the remaining Western Wall (*Kotel Ma'aravi**). Nevertheless, "wherever Israel were exiled, *shekhinah* was exiled with them." The presence of God may be revealed and embraced anywhere in the world.

Kabbalistic tradition (*Kabbalah**) sees *shekhinah* as the tenth of the *sefirot,** the link between the hidden God and lower worlds. In Kabbalistic writings, especially those stemming from the *Zohar, shekhinah* is described primarily in feminine terms, as the bride of the blessed Holy One and the Queen of the universe. Their sacred marital union (which is in fact a reunion, since they are originally one) becomes the goal of all religious life. As Kabbalists perform the commandments they dedicate their actions to "the union of blessed Holy One and His *shekhinah,* in love and fear, in the name of all Israel." The reunion of "male" and "female" within the God-head is understood as the restoration of harmony to the entire universe, allowing the flow of Divine Presence to become fully manifest throughout the world.

צמצום

Tsimtsum

THIS TERM is first used in an early *Midrash** describing the paradox of how the same God Who is everywhere, even beyond the heavens, can also be found in a specific way in the Temple or the *mishkan**: "He who fills the universe contracted His Presence to dwell between the two staves of the ark."

Later Kabbalistic (*Kabbalah**) teaching sees *tsimtsum* as God's self-contracting that took place before Creation. In order for the non-God to come into being, and so it would not be immediately re-absorbed into God, there first had to exist an empty "space" that it could occupy. Thus the first act in the creative process was God's self-contracting or "emptying" God's Self from a certain place. Divinity then sent rays of creative energy into that void, eventually bringing about the created world.

The notion of *tsimtsum* became well-known in Jewish theology through its prominence in the teachings of Rabbi Isaac Luria (1534–1572), who is also known as *ha-ARI ha-kadosh* or "the holy lion." Some interpreters of Luria's rather obscure teachings have read *tsimtsum* as a myth of the origins of evil: God's self-absenting from the void permits evil to grow its earliest roots, while God remains transcendent to that evil. Later Hasidic tradition understood *tsimtsum* primarily in a psychological sense: The human soul, a part of God above, needs "space" in order to develop its separate identity. God thus "withdraws" from the mind or becomes invisible to us, so that we have the room to become the people we need to be in order to serve God out of free choice. Some Hasidic writers insisted that this *tsimtsum* was purely illusory, that God gives humans the *illusion* that we are separate beings, while in fact all is eternally one within God.

The notion of *tsimtsum* has enjoyed a revival in recent Jewish theological writing. Certain writers have also pointed to the parallel between *tsimtsum* and aspects of contemporary astrophysics, including the "black hole" phenomenon.

תורה ותלמודה

Torah: Text and Process

Aggadah

AGGADAH means "narrative," and it refers precisely to that: the narrative traditions of classical Judaism. These include expanded and often fanciful versions of Biblical tales, stories about the lives and deeds of the early rabbis, occasional creations of pure fantasy (like the tall tales of Rabba bar bar Hanna in the *Talmud**), wise sayings, riddles, and some early bits of post-Biblical Hebrew poetry. All of this elaborate narrative and descriptive literature, preserved in the two versions of the Talmud (Babylonian and Palestinian) and in Midrashic literature, is distinguished from the prescriptive "legal" literature designated as *halakhah**, which outlines the path we are to follow through daily life.

Though in many cases *aggadah* was clearly a product of poetic imagination, later generations often took it to be literally and historically true. This created serious problems for Jewish philosophers, including Maimonides, who found it difficult to defend some of the more far-fetched creations of aggadic fantasy. One of the distinguishing hallmarks of ultra-Orthodoxy today, especially in its approach to education, is to insist on the literal truth of aggadic statements.

Of perhaps greater wisdom is the rabbinic dictum that says: "Do you want to know the One who spoke and created the world? Study *aggadah!*" It is the warm and humanizing picture of God created by the masters of *aggadah* over the centuries that gives Jews our insight into divinity. The true nature of God and the relationship of the One to the many remain ever beyond our human grasp. But the gates of imagination are ever open, and it is only through these, as cultivated in the reading and study of *aggadah*, that we dare to catch a glimpse of that which cannot be seen.

הגדה

Haggadah

THE *HAGGADAH* is the text used for the *seder**, a ritual meal ordinarily conducted at home on the first two evenings of Passover (*Pesah**).

The word *Haggadah* means "narrative," and refers to the commandment in Exodus 13:8 "to tell your child" of the liberation from slavery. One of the obligations of Passover is to hand down the tale of the Exodus from each generation to the next. This narration is to take place, according to the rabbis, while the paschal meal, including *matzah** and bitter herbs, are laid out before us.

Today's *Haggadah* text grew out of very early *Midrash**, some elements of which date back to the 1st or 2nd century B.C.E. The *Haggadah* evolved and grew over the centuries until the invention of printing halted the process, resulting in a standardization of the text. The *Haggadah* has been one of the most widely printed Hebrew books; collectors of rare *Haggadot* count thousands of editions. It is also the classic Hebrew book that has been most widely illustrated, both in illuminated manuscripts and in a variety of printings, both early and late.

While word-for-word recitation of the *Haggadah* text became the norm in most traditional households, the text ideally serves also as a springboard for discussion around the *seder* table. In order that the commandment of "telling" be fulfilled, it is required that children be included in that conversation in a way that the memory of persecution, exile, and liberation becomes meaningful to them.

Halakhah

Lord, teach me Your path
That I may walk in Your truth. (Psalm 86:11)

"WALKING IN GOD'S TRUTH" is *halakhah*, the normative path
trodden by those who wish to follow God's will, the life prescribed
by *Torah** as fulfilled in the context of real, ongoing, and evolving
human community.

Halakhah is the way to walk; it is the shortcut through the maze
of rabbinic disputation. The *Talmud** text may record the views of
one generation after another on a particular practice, including
arguments that seem to knock down all the possible courses of
action. What is a person to do? How does one act? Then, seemingly
from out of nowhere, a voice on the page will say *hilkheta* (Aramaic
for *halakhah*), meaning "action directive"; *this* is the way to go.

Halakhah comes to represent the body of such practical decisions, the ways in which a person is to act in each situation. From
early post-Talmudic times (8th century), it begins to appear in systematic compilations. These climax in the great codes of Maimonides (12th century), Jacob ben Asher (13th century), and
Joseph Caro (16th century; *Shulḥan 'Arukh**).

The ability to consult and study such codes gives to the
halakhah a fixed and somewhat rigid appearance. It becomes hard
to remember that each line in the code and each gloss in its margins is the result of a living process, decisions made by generations
of scholars (*talmid ḥakham**; *rav**) about how to understand the
Torah, where to expand its meaning, where to contract it, where to
re-apply to an entirely new area. Some of these decisions required
great moral courage. The sage staked not only his this-worldly

reputation, but even his very soul, on the legitimacy of a daring interpretation of *halakhah,* especially one that would allow more freedom, and hence risk violating the will of heaven. Other decisions, perhaps more of them, reflect the conservatism of jurists everywhere and their reluctance to set precedent or to tamper with precedent received. Such conservatism tends to grow with the system's age, and it should be no surprise that the earlier authorities were often freer to interpret and legislate than were their later successors. In recent centuries, when the halakhically observant community has seen itself as under threat, the tendency has been toward ever greater stringency. A leading contemporary Jewish thinker, David Hartman, has observed:

> *Halakhah* revolves around two poles: the legal, that is specified and detailed rules of behavior, and relational, that is, the yearning to give expression to the intimate covenantal relationship between God and Israel. Both these poles have shaped halakhic thought and practice. The legal pole, the tendency to fix formulations for conduct, may reflect the yearning and need of human beings for order and predictability in relationships. The way is given. The task of the covenantal Jew is merely to respond. On the other hand, the covenantal pole emphasizes that *halakhah* is not only a formal system concerned with rules of procedure but also an expressive system grounded in the love relationship symbolized by God's invitation to Israel to become His covenantal community. The understanding of *halakhah* as a covenantal relational experience guards against the mistaken notion that a dynamic living relationship with God can be structured exclusively by fixed and permanent rules. The need for order must not be at the expense of spontaneity, personal passion, novelty, and surprise. One committed to the halakhic system can meet God in new ways. The perennial problem that one faces in liv-

ing by *halakhah* is how to prevent the covenantal relational pole from being obscured by the massive, seemingly self-sufficient legal framework.[1]

---

1. David Hartman, "Halakhah," in Arthur Cohen and Paul Mendes-Flohr,
Contemporary Jewish Religious Thought, p. 310.

חומש

Ḥumash

A ḤUMASH is a copy of the *Torah**, or the Five Books of Moses, in the form of a printed book. The Five Books are also referred to by the Greek term Pentateuch. One does not refer to such a book as a "Torah" in order to distinguish it from the handwritten *sefer Torah* or Torah scroll, which is kept in the *aron kodesh**, the ark in the synagogue, though its contents are the same. A *ḥumash* may be printed with or without commentaries or translation.

The term *ḥumash* actually means "fifth," and its usage may derive from the time when such books were either hand copied or printed in five separate volumes. One volume at a time was given to children for study. *Ḥumash* is the beginning point of traditional Jewish education, and was the chief subject learned in *ḥeder*, the old-fashioned Jewish elementary school.

Much of Judaism's wisdom is contained in comments and homilies on the text of the *ḥumash*. Many of these are printed in the varied commentaries that accompany the text. The classic works of *Midrash** as well as the main teachings of Hasidism are presented in the form of commentaries. In fact, both are written summaries of what were originally oral discussions of the weekly Torah reading. Much of Jewish learning for adults as it is being renewed in our day is taking the form of discussions of the *ḥumash*. This reading creates old/new insights into the unchanging text that forever stands as the firm base for an ever evolving Judaism.

Kabbalah

KABBALAH literally means "the received." It refers to esoteric knowledge, secret traditions through which humans can glimpse God and have access to religious experience. The term came to have this meaning in the Middle Ages. *Kabbalah* specifically refers to the texts, practices, and doctrines of medieval Jewish mysticism and its later development. In a broader (though technically incorrect) sense, *Kabbalah* is used to refer to all Jewish esoteric or mystical teaching.

The original Kabbalistic teaching centered around the ten *sefirot** and the various symbolic guises in which they appear. The role of the *mitsvot* (*mitsvah**) as embodiments of the *sefirot* in this world is an important part of this teaching, especially as the life of Jewish practice is seen by *Kabbalah* as having cosmic or theurgic power. This notion that human actions can affect the upper world shows the root of *Kabbalah* in the ancient traditions of magic preserved in Jewish sources. "Practical *Kabbalah*," including the manipulation of holy names, the writing of amulets, protections against evil spirits, and so forth, links *Kabbalah* to this magical realm.

The greatest masters of *Kabbalah* mostly avoided these magical associations. They saw themselves involved in the more important work of sustaining the cosmos itself and bringing about its redemption. With this in mind, they focused on the union of the *sefirot,* and especially of the male and female symbolic elements within the Deity. An ascetic regimen came increasingly to be associated with *Kabbalah*, including fasting, special penances, and various ways of purging the body. These were combined with an exquisite concentration in prayer, particularly on the names of

God. This intense devotional life is lived in conjunction with study of Judaism's sacred texts, always with the hope of drawing forth new insights to be added to the store of mystical knowledge.

Kabbalah attained its greatest strength as the primary theology of Judaism in the 16th century. Eventually modernity eclipsed the role of *Kabbalah* in Western Judaism, largely because it seemed antirational, superstitious, and medieval. All these were epithets of shame among Jews seeking to assimilate into a modern, scientific, and hopefully rational world. Today, only small circles of Kabbalists, mostly of Near Eastern origin, continue to exist, primarily in Jerusalem.

In recent decades interest in *Kabbalah* has revived, and many books and classes have attempted to present Kabbalistic teaching to appeal to contemporary seekers. In many of these writings, the change is mere window dressing. The essential belief system and structure of the old *Kabbalah* are unchanged; only the metaphors and examples are updated. But if *Kabbalah* is truly going to inspire a Jewish mystical revival for our times, we must give it new meaning. The exclusive Jewish claim must give way to an understanding that *Kabbalah* is part of a worldwide retrieval of spiritual truth. The Kabbalists' emphasis on the "mystery of faith" found in the *mitsvot* must be applied to the ethical and interpersonal, as well as the ritual, commandments. A new language of *Kabbalah* should serve to enhance and spell out Judaism's essential claim that each person is the divine image and that all things contain and mask the living presence of God.

Maḥzor

THE MAHZOR is a prayer book for holiday use, especially for Rosh
Hashanah and Yom Kippur. A *maḥzor* will include special *piyyutim** or liturgical poems recited on the holiday, as well as additional readings appropriate for study and reflection on that particular day. In a traditional *maḥzor,* these will include chapters of the
mishnah* in which the particular holiday is discussed.

The term *maḥzor* comes from a verb meaning "return," which
refers to the cycle of holidays that brings us back to the beginning
of each year. *Maḥzorim* have been printed in many versions and
often incorporate local customs of various Jewish communities.

Only recently have synagogues begun to supply worshippers
with uniform *maḥzorim*. Previously, each person brought a *maḥzor*
to *shul*. Nearly every traditional household, even the poorest and
least educated, would own a *maḥzor*. In Europe these were often
published with Yiddish translations, popular commentaries filled
with pious parables, and special supplications in Yiddish that
would bring tears to the eyes of those who understood little of the
formal Hebrew liturgy.

מדרש

Midrash

THE BEST English translation for *midrash* is probably "inquiry." *Midrash* refers to the old rabbinic *method* of inquiry into the meaning of Biblical texts, as well as to the *literature* of that inquiry.

Midrashic method is a way of reading the Hebrew Bible that serves as the basis of Judaism as it was created by the rabbis in the generations following the destruction of the Second Temple (70 C.E.). It assumes divine authorship and inspiration of the entire Bible. Thus all of Scripture is kept in mind as each verse is read. The Midrashic author might take a verse from anywhere in the entire Bible to begin commenting on the verse at hand. In fact the most common tool of *midrash* is the juxtaposition of verses, based on some commonality of language or content. Other methods of interpretation are enumerated in the thirteen rules of Rabbi Ishmael (a cautious, restrictive set of rules, used for halakhic *midrash*) and the thirty-two rules of Rabbi Eliezer (a "looser" or more expansive list of rules for reading Scripture, fitting to aggadic readings). Beyond these, the Midrash assumes that rabbinic norms of attitude and behavior had existed virtually unchanged since the days of the patriarchs. This allows for projection of the authors' own values and concerns onto figures in the Biblical narrative.

The purpose of halakhic *midrash* is the justification of rabbinic legal and ritual practice by attaching it to a Scriptural base. At times the verse is truly the obvious source for the practice at hand; elsewhere the connection between them is entirely fanciful, and it is clear that the practice in question developed through an extra-Scriptural process. The rabbis are aware of such frail links between practice and Scripture and they refer to them as "mountains hanging by a hair." Nevertheless, the grounding of the entirety of

Judaism in Biblical sources was considered to be of great value. The primary collections of halakhic *midrash* are the Mekhilta on the Book of Exodus, Sifra on Leviticus, and Sifre on Numbers and Deuteronomy.

Aggadic *midrash* is an extension of the Biblical text by the canons of *aggadah*. It was practiced over many centuries, both in the Land of Israel and in the diaspora. The collections of Aggadic *midrash* range from such early classics as Genesis and Leviticus Rabbah, composed perhaps as early as the 5th century, to the Pesiktot, covering *Torah** and *haftarah** readings for special occasions, to compilations on the five *megillot** and shorter texts compiled by many medieval and modern midrashic anthologies. A *midrash* called *rabbah*, which means "great" or "large," was considered to be the major *midrash* on that particular Biblical book.

The method of midrashic interpretation has been revived in recent decades. Groups of Jews who gather in synagogues, *havurot* (*havurah**), and *minyanim* (*minyan**) engage in ongoing weekly discussion of the Torah text. These conversations are resulting in a genre of new *midrash* for our age, much of it colored by deep psychological insight into the Biblical narrative. This burst of creative energy is only beginning to find written (and more often electronic) expression. Creative *midrash* also characterizes much of the writing and teaching that takes place within Jewish feminist circles. There it is sometimes viewed as the restoration of a "lost" portion of the tradition, a women's understanding that had never been recorded in writing. The term *midrash* is also frequently used in contemporary literary criticism, referring usually to a method of literary interpretation that permits the reader, within certain criteria, to project from his or her own experience in the interpretation of texts.

מִשְׁנָה

Mishnah

THE MISHNAH is the first standardized compilation of rabbinic teaching. It was edited in the school of Rabbi Judah ha-Nasi around 220 C.E. and is devoted primarily to matters involving halakhic obligation, including religious, familial, and commercial concerns. A small portion of the text concerns *aggadah**. This is mostly concentrated in the tractate *Pirkey Avot**, or *Sayings of the Early Sages*.

The term *mishnah* comes from a Hebrew root meaning "repeat," because the compilation was originally an oral one and was committed to memory by means of frequent oral recitation. This basic document of the "Oral Law" was transferred to writing only several centuries after it was compiled.

The *Mishnah* is divided into six orders: *Zera'im* ("Seeds," referring to agricultural matters, but opening with a section on prayer); *Mo'ed* ("Occasion," referring to Sabbaths and Festivals); *Nashim* ("Women," laws of marriage, divorce, family obligation, and related matters); *Nezikin* ("Damages," including the court system, judges, oaths, property rights, debts, etc.); *Kodashim* ("Holy Things," the sacrificial system, the Temple, the priesthood, but also including a treatise on "profane" slaughter, and hence the laws of *kashrut/kosher**); and *Tohorot* ("Purities," matters of ritual purity and impurity). Within these orders, the *Mishnah* is divided into topically defined tractates, which are further subdivided into chapters. The *Mishnah* forms the basis for the later discussions that constitute the *Talmud** and thus lends its structure to the *Talmud* as a whole.

פֵּירוּשׁ, פַּרשָׁנוּת

Perush, Parshanut

PERUSH means "commentary"; *parshanut* is the act of writing a commentary or the collective field of commentary literature.

No literary form is as characteristic of Judaism as the commentary. From earliest post-Biblical times, Jewish writings have taken the form of commentaries on the Biblical text. This process actually begins within the Bible itself, where later writers take up themes written by earlier authors and comment, often by restructuring or by subtle changes of context. The Dead Sea Scrolls, written mostly in the 2nd century B.C.E., already include Biblical commentaries, showing that commentary was well under way as the Biblical era drew to a close.

The literature of *Midrash** is the first major stratum of Jewish Bible commentary. Parallel and mostly contemporaneous with it is *targum*, a series of Aramaic translations and paraphrases of the text that contain important elements of commentary.

The early Middle Ages marked an attempt by Jews (partly due to Arabic cultural influence) to escape the fanciful interpretations of *Midrash* and get back to *peshat,* the plain meaning or simple intent of Scripture. Here the literature known as *parshanut* began to develop, including the most famous commentaries of the French rabbi Solomon Isaaci (1040–1105), also known as RaSHI; Rabbi Abraham Ibn Ezra, a Spaniard who later also lived in France and Italy (1089–1164); and the Spanish Rabbi Moses ben Naḥman (1194–1270), also called RaMBaN. Hundreds of lesser-known authors wrote commentaries in this period as well. Only a few of the most prolific writers commented on all or nearly all of Scripture; most wrote commentaries on the *Torah**, one or more of the five scrolls (*megillah**), or another Biblical book of special significance.

As both *Talmud** and *Midrash* came to be seen as sacred texts, they too became the subject of commentaries. Talmudic commentaries often began with notes written by a scholar in the margins of his copy of a particular tractate, perhaps intended primarily for his own use. These would be published, by disciples or by owners of later printing houses, as commentaries. The prayer book and especially the Passover *haggadah** were also favorites of commentators.

As time went on, commentaries themselves often seemed to be in need of explanation, and they too became the objects of commentary. Such works, known as supercommentaries, are very common among later traditional Jewish writings.

The form of commentary often served a dual and somewhat contradictory purpose. Writing a commentary on a work is an act of validation; it indicates that the original work is still important and worthy of study. At the same time, that work is re-interpreted by the commentator, who may feel free to insert many new ideas into it through the guise of interpretation. The ongoing process of commentary thus served as Judaism's best vehicle for continuous cultural creativity, while maintaining the theoretical framework of its classic sources and their unchallenged status as sources of authority.

As you write your own notes in the margins and white spaces of this book, as I encourage you to do, you will be engaging in this ancient Jewish art of commentary. Who knows? Perhaps some future generation will rediscover your work and publish it, adding your words to the long and unbroken chain of tradition, "the great voice that never ceases."

פרקי אבות
Pirkey Avot

Avot (literally "fathers" or "ancestors," though referring here to the "founders" of rabbinic tradition) is a unique tractate within the *Mishnah** that records wise sayings, maxims, and teachings of the most notable pharisees and *tanna'im*. These were the teachers and rabbis of the late Second Temple and Mishnaic period (100 B.C.E. to 220 C.E.).

The tractate opens with a statement that may be seen as an introduction to the *Mishnah* as a whole: "Moses received *Torah** from Sinai, passing it on to Joshua, who passed it on to the elders, who passed it on to the prophets, who passed it to the members of the Great Assembly." The Great Assembly is the origin of the Sanhedrin, the high court that still existed in Mishnaic times. The rabbis are claiming, in other words, that their authority derives by this direct chain from what Moses received at Sinai. Some scholars believe that this tractate was once located at the very end of the *Mishnah* as a justification of the entire text.

The actual sayings of the rabbis in *Avot* are quite distinctive within rabbinic literature. They are neither *halakhah** nor the ordinary sort of narrative *aggadah**. They belong essentially to the Wisdom tradition, collections of maxims and wise sayings represented earlier by the Biblical book of Proverbs and the apocryphal Ben Sira. Sometimes they even seem to have a Hellenistic flavor. The actual historical connection between each figure and the saying(s) attributed to him is impossible to determine.

Over time, *Avot* became a favorite text for the teaching of morals. Many of its maxims are known by heart and are often remembered and quoted in the context of conversation about ethical matters. *Avot* is recited or taught in the synagogue, primarily on *shabbat** afternoons during the summer months. Because one chapter was studied each week, the chapters of this text came to be known as *Pirkey Avot, "Chapters"* or *Sayings of the Early Sages.*

פִּיּוּט

Piyyut

Piyyut, an old Hebrew term for "poem," refers to poetic works or hymns that are recited within the liturgy of the synagogue. The word *piyyut* is actually derived from the Greek and is related to our English word "poet."

The *piyyut* tradition dates back to the 6th or 7th century and began in the Land of Israel. The liturgical text was much less fixed than it later came to be, and poets were allowed, when leading communal prayers, to recite their own compositions that were appropriate to the liturgical theme of the day or hour. A body of these poems was built up over many centuries. Some *piyyutim* are of known authorship (due to the common use of alphabetical acrostics, where the author's name was woven into the opening letter of each line or stanza) and others are anonymous. Local custom eventually chose one or another for regular recitation. In this way, there developed various liturgical traditions that included particular groups of *piyyutim.* Some of these practices became uniform over vast areas, such as the Eastern Ashkenazic rite, which prayer books often described as that of "Poland, Lithuania, Bohemia, and Moravia," while others were quite localized, such as the unique *piyyutim* that used to be recited in Worms, Germany or in Carpentras/Avignon in France.

Piyyutim were usually composed and recited for special occasions in the sacred year. These include *Rosh Hashanah** and *Yom Kippur**, the three pilgrimage festivals (*Pesaḥ**, *Shavu'ot**, and *Sukkot**), the four special sabbaths leading up to *Pesaḥ,* and various other events. In modern times *piyyutim,* which are often lengthy and difficult to understand, have been eliminated by many synagogues and prayer books. But they are still worthy of reading and study. The ingenious authors often had to create new Hebrew words (out of old roots) to fulfill their highly exacting demands for alphabetical, acrostic, and rhymed verse. *Piyyutim* are an endless font of information about Hebrew language and midrashic traditions. They are still to be found in the traditional *maḥzor** for *Rosh Hashanah* and *Yom Kippur*. Some recent *maḥzorim* include selections of modern poetry in place of the old *piyyutim*.

 Sefer

SEFER is the word for "book" in Hebrew; the Jews are 'Am ha-Sefer, the People of the Book. That title, incidentally, first given to us many centuries ago by the Muslims (showing their respect for the Hebrew Bible), was one we accepted proudly.

In Yiddish a distinction is made between a *bukh*, an ordinary book, and a *sefer*, a holy book. *Sefer* in that context may refer to a *Torah** scroll, to a commentary, a legal compilation, or even a collection of your rabbi's latest sermons. There are rules of proper conduct with regard to a *sefer*: It should not be left open when unused; it should never be placed on the floor and should be picked up and kissed if it falls; it should always lie right-side-up on a table. The *sefer* should be revered as one would honor a teacher, since it contains the living word of God.

שיר השירים

Shir ha-Shirim

SHIR HA-SHIRIM, the Song of Songs, sometimes referred to as the "Song of Solomon" or "Canticles," is a Biblical book comprising poems of love and marriage spoken between a shepherd and shepherdess of ancient Israel. Numerous references to King Solomon in the text, as well as to the walls, towers, streets, and markets of Jerusalem caused the book to be attributed to him.

At first glance, the presence of this book within the *tanakh** is surprising. It never refers to God and the eros of its verses is quite unabashed. In fact the holy character of this work was long debated and it was one of the last books to be included within Scripture. Rabbi Akiva, the great sage and martyr of the 2nd century, was its champion. He said that "all the writings [of Scripture] are holy, but the Song of Songs is the holy of holies; the entire world is not worthy of the day when *Shir ha-Shirim* was given to Israel." That day, according to Rabbi Akiva, was the day of Sinai itself. Akiba was Judaism's greatest believer in love as the basis of all religion. He saw *Shir ha-Shirim* as the heart of God's *Torah**, the declaration of mutual love between God and His people that forms the only true basis for all the rest of Jewish living.

Shir ha-Shirim is an especially beloved text in the Jewish mystical tradition. There is hardly a page in the *Zohar*, the greatest work of the *Kabbalah**, that does not comment on some verse of the Song. The hills, gardens, and perfumed fountains of *Shir ha-Shirim* are all turned into symbols in the *Zohar*. They are taken to represent the powerful spiritual attraction of the *sefirot** to one another and to their hidden source. But they also set the stage for the intoxicating inner journey of the mystics themselves, who play a key role in this great act of cosmic union.

It is the custom of Sephardic and Hasidic Jews to recite the entire Song of Songs each Friday night, before the *Kabbalat Shabbat** service. As one of the five *megillot*, it is read in the synagogue on the intermediate Sabbath of *Pesah*.

שֻׁלְחָן עָרוּך

Shulḥan 'Arukh

THE SHULḤAN 'ARUKH or "Set Table" is a codification of Jewish law (halakhah*) written by Rabbi Joseph Caro (1488–1575). It was first published in Venice in 1564. The Shulḥan 'Arukh came to be accepted as the "last word" of Jewish legal authority, and contemporary rabbis still follow its guidance in determining norms of behavior. They refer to it even in response to modern inventions and societal changes that could not have been imagined by its author.

The structure of the Shulḥan 'Arukh follows that of an earlier compilation of laws, the Arba'ah Turim or Four Columns of Rabbi Jacob ben Asher. Its four parts are the Oraḥ Ḥayyim or "Path of Life," which deals with ritual behavior throughout the Jewish calendar year; Yoreh De'ah or "Teacher of Knowledge," on laws of kashrut (kosher*), mourning, and other areas of religious practice; Even ha-'Ezer or "The Helpmate," laws of marriage, divorce, and the status of women; and Ḥoshen Mishpat, "The Breastplate of Judgment," the civil and criminal codes. Caro's Shulḥan 'Arukh is essentially a distillation of the rulings found in his Bet Yosef, a commentary on the Arba'ah Turim.

Caro was a Sephardic Jew and his rulings reflect the practice of the Mediterranean-based Sephardic communities of his day. His work was adapted for use in the Ashkenazic communities by Rabbi Moses Isserles, whose brief glosses are called the Mappah ("Tablecloth") and are always published alongside Caro's text.

The Shulḥan 'Arukh should not be confused with another work called Kitsur Shulḥan 'Arukh ("The Little Set Table") by Rabbi Solomon Ganzfried. This work, widely available in English under the title Code of Jewish Law, features the most stringent and sometimes extreme views of 19th-century Hungarian rabbis.

סדור

Siddur

A *siddur* is a prayer book, a printed or written text of the fixed prayer service for ordinary weekdays and Sabbaths (*Shabbat**). It is distinguished from a *maḥzor**, which contains prayers for the holiday cycle.

The word *siddur* means "order"; this indicates that the prayers are laid out in their proper order for use in the service. The oldest Hebrew prayer book texts we have were created by Rabbi Amram Gaon (who died around 875) and Rabbi Saadia Gaon (882–942). Concern with the proper ordering of prayers and blessings characterizes some of the earliest rabbinic discussions of prayer, and the term *siddur* reflects that concern.

There are two primary versions of the *siddur* text: the Ashkenazic, used by Jews from central and eastern Europe, and the Sephardic, used by Jews descended from the Spanish exiles, living around the Mediterranean, especially in the countries of the old Turkish empire, as well as other oriental Jewish communities. In fact there are several more subsets and varieties of Jewish liturgy than just these two. Italian, Yemenite, and other communities each have their own ancient and distinctive *siddur*. The prayer book used by Hasidic Jews, which is called *Nusaḥ Sepharad*, in fact combines Sephardic, Ashkenazic, and some original Hasidic traditions.

In early synagogues, it was assumed that worshippers knew by heart the prayers they were required to say. In some situations prayers were repeated after the leader or called out as responses. This served as an aid to oral recitation. Manuscript prayer books, perhaps the property of synagogues or communities, sometimes with illuminated decoration, were highly prized possessions in the Middle Ages. There is no indication that prayer books were in the hands of ordinary worshippers before the invention of printing.

From the 16th century onward, the *siddur* came to be the most frequently printed and widely distributed Hebrew text. Printing houses in places like Amsterdam, Sulzbach (in Bavaria, for the South German communities), and Livorno, Italy became famous for their constant supply of *siddurim*, first in Hebrew and later with translations into other languages. In Eastern Europe, Vilna, Warsaw, and Piotrkow supplied most of the *siddurim* until the Holocaust. The *siddur* with English translation has been published in countless editions, primarily in London and New York.

Changes in the *siddur* text constituted one of the earliest features of Reform Judaism. Since the early 19th century, each non-Orthodox denomination has frequently issued updated versions of the *siddur*. These serve as much as emblems of the movements' ideologies as they do as aids to the community of worshippers.

תַּלְמוּד

Talmud

THE *TALMUD*, literally "the learning," is the great Jewish compendium of law, wisdom, folklore, and everyday life from the early centuries of the common era. It takes the form of an abbreviated report of rabbinic discussions around the *Mishnah**, from the time that text was edited (about 220 C.E.) through the 5th century. The *Talmud* exists in two versions, the Babylonian and Palestinian. The latter is also called the "Jerusalem *Talmud*." The Babylonian is a fuller text and includes lengthier discussion, especially of the civil code. Since the early Middle Ages it has been considered the more authoritative version.

The rabbis whose voices are most prominent in the *Talmud* are those who taught and studied in the great academies. In the Land of Israel these were in Tiberias, Sepphoris, and Caesaria; in Babylonia they were in Sura, Pumbedita, and Nehardea. In each of these academies the *Mishnah*, still an orally preserved code, was taught and its authority promulgated. Alongside the codified *Mishnah* text, oral tradition also preserved large numbers of other early teachings, known as *beraitot* or "external" teachings. ("External" simply means that these teachings had not been selected for inclusion by the editors of the *Mishnah*.) As a *Mishnah* passage was taught and discussed, challenges to it were encouraged. These might be based on opposing *beraitot,* on supposed inner contradictions in the *Mishnah* text, and (especially in the Babylonian schools) on assumed principles of logic and common sense. The *Talmud* defends the *Mishnah* as best it can, but not infrequently it emends or significantly re-interprets the *Mishnah* text in order to conform to objections found to be worthy.

The "oral stenography" that recorded these discussions often encapsulates several centuries of conversation in a single page. Later layers in the discussion may find contradictions with principles of law that had been articulated by prior generations, sometimes when dealing with entirely different subject matter. Despite the different context, the principle seems to apply. The discussion may then veer off course, including a few lines or even a whole page relating to that other subject, perhaps re-testing the principle before applying it here. Several other ancillary cases may also be brought to bear in that context before the discussion returns to the matter originally at hand. Thus it is that a page of *Talmud* might contain materials as early as the 1st century and as late as the 5th century, with its content ranging through the widest conceivable array of areas that interested the rabbis or represented daily life in their time.

Talmud came to be the central text of Jewish learning. Study of the *Talmud* requires mastery of its terse interrogative style, its unique linguistic combination of Hebrew and Babylonian Aramaic, the associative patterns by which seemingly unrelated subjects are drawn together, as well as the vast array of topics actually discussed among the rabbis. Such study is classically carried on by pairs or small groups of learners (*evruta*). In such a setting, the interrogative and dialogic style of the text can best be preserved. *Talmud* study, while difficult and often abstruse in content, is seen by the true *talmid ḥakham** as a labor of love and the source of great joy. The completion of a tractate is an occasion for celebration. A *siyyum ha-shas*, or a completion of the entire *Talmud*, is a truly rare and great event in the life of one devoted to Jewish learning.

Tanakh

THE *TANAKH* is the Hebrew Bible. *TaNaKh* is an acronym formed by the first letters of the three sections of the Bible, according to the traditional Hebrew division: *Torah**, *Nevi'im* or "Prophets," and *Ketuvim* or "Writings" (in Greek: *hagiographia* or "holy writings"). The ordering of Scripture in this way reflects both the relative dates of canonization of the various sections and the degree of divine origin attributed to each.

The *Torah** text, which was canonized in the early Second Temple period (perhaps around 450 B.C.E.), is seen as originating in the divine revelation to Moses. The books of the prophets include the historical narratives called "former prophets" and the actual prophecies in the "latter" or literary prophetic books. These are spoken in the name of God; their literal revelation to the prophet is assumed in the later tradition, though the understanding of this revelation may vary. The prophets' role in the wording of their message is not entirely denied. The Writings are a mixed bag, but they are generally seen as being written by humans who were divinely inspired by the holy spirit (*ruah ha-kodesh**).

The *Tanakh* represents the literary and religious legacy of the Israelite people over the course of their development, a period stretching for more than a thousand years. In the earliest part of that period, tales now included in the Biblical text were told orally. These were developed and refined when committed to writing. Some of the oldest texts in the *Tanakh* are poems such as the Song at the Sea (Exodus 15) or Deborah's Song (Judges 5). When handing down poetry, transmitters felt less free to tamper with received formulations. As Israelite culture matured, a variety of literary works were composed in Hebrew, including historical writings,

legal texts, prophecies, Psalms, and wisdom treatises. The latest
text within the *Tanakh* is the Book of Daniel, an apocalypse written
near the time of the Macabbean revolt (165 B.C.E.). All of these
were joined together in the ongoing canonization process that
determined which books were to be considered holy and worthy of
preservation.

The *Tanakh* is the fount out of which all later Judaism grows.
The self-image of rabbinic and later Judaism is one of complete
faithfulness to Scripture. Even though there are divergences from
Biblical practice in many areas (the substitution of liturgical prayer
for animal sacrifice is one obvious example), these are usually
justified by recourse to the Biblical text itself. Judaism throughout
its history has developed around an ongoing process of Scriptural
interpretation. Though always nominally faithful to the text, later
Judaism was often far from literalist in its understandings of the
Bible. Both *Midrash* * and later *parshanut* * offered room for a great
variety of readings, many of which restricted or transformed the
authority with which the text was to be vested.

While Judaism has always considered the entire *Tanakh* to be
holy, the emphasis placed on one book or another has varied with
changes in time and interest. *Kabbalah* * raised the interest in the
Song of Songs (*Shir ha-Shirim* *). Hasidic Judaism tended to focus
on the *ḥumash* *, the portion best known to simple Jews. Zionist
educators revived interest in the former prophets, replete with
tales of Israel's early life in *Erets Yisrael* *. Reform Judaism redis-
covered the latter prophets, long known from *haftarah* * chanting
but otherwise sadly neglected. Future generations and new visions
of Judaism will undoubtedly make their own choices within the
richness and variety of ancient Hebrew Scripture.

Tehillim

TEHILLIM are Psalms, the 150 sacred songs contained in *Sefer Tehillim* or the Biblical Psalter, traditionally ascribed to King David. The singular form is *tehillah*, but the more commonly used word to designate a single Psalm is *mizmor*, which means "song."

After the *ḥumash**, *tehillim* is the best-known and most widely quoted book of the Bible in Jewish literature. The spiritual life of Judaism is formed around the central themes of the Psalter: singing to God as the author of Creation, praising God's saving power as manifest both to the individual and the community of Israel, crying out to God in pain and loneliness. It is also the most important model for all of Hebrew religious poetry until modern times. Almost half of the *tehillim* are known by heart by many traditionally observant Jews because they are recited frequently as a part of the regular liturgy. These include the *pesukey de-zimrah*, the Psalms assigned to conclude the morning service on each day of the week, the eight Psalms of the *Kabbalat Shabbat** or "welcoming the Sabbath" service, and the Psalms of *hallel**.

Among traditionally pious Ashkenazic Jews, daily or weekly recitation of *tehillim* is considered to be of great merit. The *tehillim-yid* (literally, "Psalm Jew") who recites extra *tehillim* each day is usually a person of little learning but great enthusiasm. While the more learned may gather after prayers to study the *Talmud**, those with less knowledge will take the time to express their piety by the more emotional vehicle of reciting *gants tehillim*, the entire Book of Psalms.

תחינות

Teḥinot

Teḥinot are "supplications," prayers that directly call out for divine intervention in the daily life of this world. They are not a part of the fixed and required liturgy and undoubtedly arose as a spontaneous counterpoint to the grandeur of liturgical prayer, especially as it was understood by the Kabbalists (*Kabbalah**). Eventually such spontaneous outcries also came to be written down and preserved as texts. These are known as *teḥinot*.

Teḥinot are primarily identified as women's prayers, and the collections of *teḥinot* that were published in the 18th and 19th century in Central and Eastern Europe, written in Yiddish, were clearly directed toward female readership. The prayers, which are most often composed in the first person feminine voice, ask for God's protection for "me, my husband, my children" and so forth. Many of the *teḥinot* are associated with dramatic events in the liturgical cycle, especially moments that are likely to be significant to women: the weekly Sabbath candlelighting, the blessing for the new month, the various moments of worship on *Rosh Hashanah** and *Yom Kippur**. Many of the *teḥinot* purport to have been written by women, but some of these female names may be pen names for male authors.

Teḥinot written for men, mostly in Hebrew, tend to exist more in Italian and Sephardic tradition, where they are sometimes referred to as *bakkashot* ("petitions"). In some communities these are chanted by special societies, much as Psalms (*tehillim**) are chanted by pious Jews of Eastern European origin.

תורה

Torah

TORAH is Judaism's most sacred word, except for the names of God. It means "teaching," and it is derived from a Hebrew root that also means "to shoot" or "to reach the mark." Torah embraces a wide range of meanings. Sometimes it refers to the very specific teachings of ancient Judaism, while at other times it embraces any true teachings to be found in the world, all of which are said to derive from a single Source.

In its narrowest sense, the word is used to refer to the Five Books of Moses, the *ḥumash** or Pentateuch. But examining the first four books of the Torah, we find no indication that this is its title. The word Torah is used quite frequently in these books, but always to indicate a specific teaching concerning one practice or another. The frequently repeated injunction to have a single Torah for citizen and stranger (Exodus 12:49 etc.) is best translated as "way of doing things." Only in Deuteronomy (4:44, 33:4), the fifth book of the Torah, does one get a sense of Torah indicating a compilation, and there it seems to refer to this fifth book itself. The first references to Torah that include some version of the text as we know it may be those of Nehemiah 8, written after the return to Zion (from the Babylonian exile) in the 5th century B.C.E. This account reflects the earliest appearance of an edited and authoritative Torah text.

Rabbinic Judaism does not admit to that development. The rabbis understand the entire five-book Torah to be God's gift to Moses. In the early rabbinic or tannaitic period (1st to early 3rd centuries) there is still some debate about how and when this revelation took place. Some envisioned revelation as a single, transformative event: The heavens opened at Sinai and all was revealed. Moses was given the history of humanity since Creation and was told of Israel's fortunes through his own death, which concludes the Torah text. One legend has it that the last eight verses of Deuteronomy, beginning "Moses the servant of the Lord died there . . ." were written in Moses' tears rather than in ink.

But other, perhaps less apocalyptic, versions of revelation were also taught. Some said that only the Ten Commandments were given at Sinai. Other laws were revealed, bit by bit, throughout the forty years in the wilderness. In most of these cases the divine voice spoke only to Moses, not to all of Israel. (Might he have misheard, just occasionally?) Deuteronomy was indeed taught by Moses just before his death, as the text itself proclaims. The entire Torah text was authoritative, according to these views, but it was not the result of a single revelatory event.

These debates were set aside in the later rabbinic or amoraic period (3rd to 6th centuries), when the grandest notions of revelation were given full sway. Moses received not only the entire Written Torah at Sinai, but the Oral Torah, the tradition of interpreting the text, as well. "Everything a faithful student was ever to say was already given to Moses at Sinai," proclaims the *Talmud**. To deny that even a single word or letter of Torah was divine constituted blasphemy.

Judaism's openness to continuing religious creativity turns on the notion of the rabbis' authority to interpret the text. Since that authority itself comes from Sinai, it cannot be questioned. But the process of interpretation opens the text to multiple readings: Aggadic (*aggadah**), halakhic (*halakhah**), grammatical, philosophic, and mystical currents of thought have all been applied to Torah throughout the ages. These add constant new levels of richness and subtlety to our understanding of it. In this way Judaism remains a highly faithful text-based tradition without becoming fundamentalist, since each text is always open to a multitude of interpretations. "The Torah has seventy faces" is a well-known saying, meaning that there are a great many legitimate ways to understand the same verse. Literalism is generally not privileged over other ways of reading.

Mystical and Hasidic Judaism tend to emphasize the notion of continuing revelation. Sinai was not just a one-time historical experience, but is one that can be renewed at any time for the person who is properly attuned to hearing. "Every day a voice goes forth from Mount Horeb saying 'Return, O humans!'" Such revelation may not contradict *halakhah*, to be sure, but it may strengthen and renew the faith of those who seek it. For most Jews, the best place to seek further revelation is within the text itself, so that the processes of study, interpretation, discovery of new meanings, and "revelation" are quite inseparable from one another.

From earliest times the rabbis insisted that Torah existed in a cosmic dimension far beyond that of Sinai and human revelation. "God looked into Torah to create the world," says the *Midrash**, reflecting still older traditions about Wisdom as the companion of God before Creation. The relationship between this eternal Torah (Did it have words? Letters? Where was it written?) and the text before us is also a matter of longstanding mystical speculation. Could it be that our Torah is only one of the "seventy faces" of God's teaching, which is itself beyond words and language? How do we trace the way back from revealed to hidden? How do we get from the very worldly concerns of *halakhah* back to the sublime yet elusive "perfect teaching of *Y-H-W-H**" (Psalm 19:8)?

דרכי העבודה
Religious Practice

עמידה

'Amidah

'AMIDAH literally means "standing." It refers to the central prayer of Jewish worship, a group of blessings (*berakhah**) to be recited thrice daily while standing, without movement or distraction. It is the core of the *shaharit** and *minhah** services and is added on to the evening recitation of the *shema'** to form the *'arvit** service. Because the weekday *'amidah* originally contained eighteen blessings (there are now nineteen), it is also known popularly as *shmoneh-'esrey* (literally, "eighteen").

The rabbis determined that standing is the most proper position for prayer from various Biblical precedents. "Abraham was yet standing before the Lord" (Genesis 18:22) when he prayed for the people of Sodom; God said to Moses "You stand here with Me" (Deuteronomy 5:28) after the people dispersed following the revelation at Sinai. Standing is also proper behavior in the presence of royalty: A humble petitioner stands before the king (*melekh**). Also related to the metaphor of God as royal personage is the practice of preceding and following petitions (the thirteen blessings in the middle of the weekday *'amidah* have a petitionary character) with statements of glorification and praise.

The three introductory and three concluding blessings of the *'amidah* constitute its oldest section, dating to late Second Temple times. On Sabbaths (*Shabbat**) and holidays only one blessing is inserted between these, thanking God for the gift of that holy day. On *Rosh Hashanah**, three are inserted. On weekdays the thirteen petitions, supposedly dating to the Yavneh period, which immediately followed the Temple's destruction in 70 C.E., are recited. The discrepancy between the traditional and the actual number of these probably results from the addition of an extra blessing in anticipation of the messiah (*mashiaḥ**). This was originally a part of the prayer for the restoration of Jerusalem.

The *'amidah* was originally a communal, rather than individual, prayer. It was recited aloud by a prayer leader, with the community responding "Amen!" to each of his blessings. Only later did it come to be recited quietly by each individual, and then repeated aloud by the leader. But the recitation of the "quiet *shmoneh-'esrey*" became the most characteristic form of Jewish devotion, and its words are deeply personalized and recited with great intensity by serious practitioners of Jewish prayer. The word *tefillah** or "prayer" itself, when found in halakhic sources, refers to this prayer alone. It is while saying the *'amidah* that our heart opens and our most private longings comingle with the ancient words to create a thoroughly Jewish and yet thoroughly personal prayer.

עַרְבִית, מַעֲרִיב

'Arvit, Ma'ariv

'ARVIT is the evening service, the last of the three services of the solar day (or, if you count the days from sunset, the first). The 'arvit service is to be recited any time between sunset and dawn. Traditionally (because of the principle "the faithful are eager to perform commandments"), it is recited in the early evening.

The original core of the 'arvit service is the shema'*, which is to be recited "when you lie down and when you rise up" (Deuteronomy 6:7). The evening shema' is surrounded by four blessings (berakhah*); two are recited before the shema' and two after it. In early times these constituted the entire statutory evening service. The 'amidah*, recited mornings and afternoons, parallel to the two daily sacrifices in the Temple, was not recited in the evening. Once the 'amidah became a form of private as well as public prayer, however, its voluntary recitation was added to the evening service. This private recitation (there is no public repetition of the 'amidah at this service) eventually came to be seen as obligatory and is considered so by halakhic authorities.

On Friday evenings and the eve of festivals (except for Shavu'ot*), it is permitted to start the evening service early, even before sundown, so as to "add on to the holy from the profane." On Saturday evenings and the conclusion of festivals, 'arvit must not be recited until the stars are seen, so as not to diminish full celebration of the holy day.

בְּרָכָה, בָּרוּךְ

Berakhah, Barukh

A BERAKHAH or "blessing" is the most classic and best-known form of Jewish prayer. Tradition claims that a pious Jew should recite at least a hundred blessings each day. The recitation of the three daily services plus the blessings before and after meals is likely to get one close to that number.

A blessing begins with the formula: *barukh atah* adonai* elohenu melekh* ha-'olam* (see also *elohim*, 'olam**). This is best translated "Blessed are You, Lord our God, universal Sovereign." (You will notice that almost all the words of the formula are explained in this book, offering you a good way to begin thinking about the concepts involved in a *berakhah*.) Longer blessings also have a concluding formula: "Blessed are You, Lord. . ." followed by the specific subject of the blessing ("Blessed are You, O Lord, Creator of lights" or "Blessed are You, O Lord, Who makes the Sabbath holy").

The word *barukh* ("blessed") is especially interesting. When we bless people (the same term is used), we bestow something upon them. We give them our good wishes as a gift, as something that will offer them strength or consolation. When we ask God to bless us, or bless one another through the priestly blessing (*dukhan**), we hope to receive of God's gifts. But here, in our most oft-repeated form of prayer, we use the same words, as though we *give* God our blessing. We know full well that God has no need of our offerings. But still, we want to give. To say *barukh* is to say that we want to add something to the wholeness that is God. In return for the endless blessings we receive, we seek, however inadequately, to be active givers in the balance of blessing upon which our universe stands.

Barukh is also traditionally related to the word *berekh,* which means "knee." It is when we recite the word *barukh* in the opening and closing of the first and next-to-last blessings of the *'amidah** that we bend our knees. This act of submission at first glance may seem to contradict the notion of giving. If we are giving to God, wouldn't we want to stretch forth and reach toward the heavens? Right here lies the mystery of faith: It is in submission that we stretch forth; in bending our knees we reach out to God.

דאַװען, דאַװנען
Daven, Davnen

Daven is the usual Yiddish word for "to recite prayers." It refers specifically to the Jewish style of worship, where each word of the prayer text is spoken, either quietly in private prayer or aloud in chant.

The word *daven* is used only by Jews of Eastern European origin. While very widespread in later Yiddish (and Judeo-English), it makes its first textual appearances among Lithuanian Jews in the 16th and 17th centuries. Many theories have been offered to explain the origins of this term, which is not cognate to any usage in German, Hebrew, or any of the Slavic languages, which are the usual roots of Yiddish. Some have tried to relate it either to Latin *divinus* ("divinity") or to the English "dawn."

A most interesting (though unproven) theory connects *daven* to a similar-sounding Lithuanian word meaning "gift." The claim is that the word is a direct Lithuanian translation of the Hebrew *minḥah**, the afternoon service, but literally meaning "offering" or "gift." Of the three daily prayer services, so the theory goes, only the *minḥah* prayers often had to be recited in public, when Jews in the marketplace were seen praying by their non-Jewish neighbors. In the course of excusing themselves for prayer or explaining to their neighbors or customers what they were doing, Jews hit upon the word *daven*, a literal translation of *minḥah*. Over the years it was incorporated into Yiddish speech.

This is an interesting theory. In any case, it carries with it the very Jewish notion that prayer replaces sacrifice and that to pray is, in fact, to give a gift, to make a verbal offering to God. The heart becomes an altar.

דוכן, דוכנען
Dukhan, Dukhnen

DUKHAN literally means a "platform" or a "stand." It refers here to the raised platform on which the *kohanim* or priests are to stand while blessing the people. *Dukhnen,* in Yiddish, is the recital of the priestly blessing by the *kohanim.*

The threefold priestly blessing found in Numbers 6:22–27 is one of the Jewish people's oldest sacred texts. It is the only such text of which written fragments have been found that date to the times of Solomon's Temple. The blessing of the people by this formula was a key part of Temple worship. Receiving this blessing was an important reason for pilgrimage to Jerusalem in ancient times.

After the Second Temple was destroyed, recital of the priestly blessing continued in the synagogue. In most services it is recited by the regular prayer leader, and in modern liberal synagogues, it is often spoken by the rabbi. It is also used by parents to bless their children at the *Shabbat** table. But there are special times in the traditional synagogue (among Ashkenazim outside Israel, on major festivals) when the descendants of the ancient priesthood still recite the blessing. Their ability to serve as channels of blessing is treated with great seriousness and the moment of *dukhnen,* or the priests' rising to the platform, is one of special awe. People traditionally cover their heads with the *tallit** so they will not look upon the priests as they convey God's blessing. The *kohanim* themselves must prepare by washing their hands and removing their shoes. They act in this way as though the Temple were still standing. Although the efficacy of the blessing does not depend upon the priest's personal piety, many *kohanim* who are not traditionally observant will refrain from ascending the *dukhan* lest they be unworthy to this last surviving holy task of Israel's ancient priesthood.

In *Erets Yisra'el** the blessing is recited by the *kohanim* on each Sabbath and in Jerusalem, site of the original Temple, it is recited every day.

הפטרה

Haftarah

THE HAFTARAH is a reading from the prophetic books of the Bible (*tanakh**) that follows the *Torah** reading in the synagogue on Sabbaths (*Shabbat**) and festivals. There is usually some relationship between the Torah and *haftarah* passages, though the connection is sometimes obscure and hence the subject of many a sermon by rabbis or *bnai mitsvah* (*bar/bat mitsvah**).

The term *haftarah* means "dismissal" or "completion," since it was the passage that came at the end of the longer Torah reading and lesson. *Haftarot* were in use by the 3rd or 4th century C.E., as witnessed by early *Midrash** that connects Torah readings to various prophetic passages. The choice of specific prophetic texts to be used as *haftarot* for each occasion is, however, a matter of custom rather than entirely fixed law. This is witnessed by the many variations between Ashkenazic and Sephardic tradition in this realm, and even by varying customs of individual communities.

The reader of the *haftarah* is known as the *maftir,* the one who completes the Torah reading. The *maftir* is called for a final *'aliyah* to read from the Torah. This *'aliyah* is additional to the minimum number of *'aliyot* required for that day. It is followed by the *maftir*'s chanting of the prophetic passage.

הלל

Hallel

HALLEL (literally "praise") is a collection of joyful Psalms that correspond to Psalms 113–118 in the Biblical text. *Hallel* is seen as a distinctive liturgical unit that is opened and followed by a blessing. It is recited on festive occasions in the course of the year. These include *Pesaḥ**, *Shavu'ot**, *Sukkot**, *Shemini Atseret** and *Simḥat Torah**, *Hanukkah**, and *Rosh Ḥodesh**. It is chanted communally and a wide array of joyous tunes are used for it.

On the six latter days of Passover and the New Moon, certain sections of Psalms 115 and 116 are omitted. This abbreviated text is called the "half *hallel*." It is used on the New Moon because that is only a "half holiday," one on which work is permitted, and on the latter days of Passover, according to ancient *Midrash**, out of deference to God's sadness at the death of the Egyptians, who were also God's children. *Hallel* is not recited on *Rosh Hashanah** and *Yom Kippur**, since those are times of judgment when the merriness of *hallel* would be inappropriate.

Hallel is also recited on Passover eve as the conclusion to the *seder**. It is accompanied by Psalm 136, referred to as "the great *hallel*," and used also in the liturgy for Sabbath (*Shabbat**) and festival mornings. Hasidic custom also encourages singing *hallel* while baking *matzot* (*matzah**) on the day preceding Passover. Many synagogues have also added *hallel* to the liturgy on the 5th of Iyyar (late April or early May on the secular calendar), in religious celebration of Israel's Independence Day.

Havdalah

HAVDALAH literally means "separation" or "distinction." It refers to the concluding ceremony or declaration of *Shabbat** that separates the holy Sabbath from ordinary weekday time and consciousness.

Havdalah is a blessing (*berakhah**) that praises God for distinguishing holy from profane. This refers not only to holy and profane time, but also to distinctions between light and dark, day and night, and Israel and other nations.

Havdalah at the end of *Shabbat* is recited over a full cup of wine, which parallels the *kiddush** when the Sabbath begins. To this symbol of fullness and joy are added two other blessings. One is recited over the smell of fragrant spices, in order to restore the soul that is faint because *Shabbat* is departing (*neshamah yeterah**). The other is over light, usually in the form of a brightly burning multiwicked candle. The *Midrash** says that Adam, at the conclusion of the first Sabbath, became frightened when he saw darkness encroaching and feared that the world would be dark forever. God consoled him by giving him the gift of fire. This first divine gift and our gratitude for it are thus renewed each Saturday evening as *Shabbat* departs and we have to face the "darkness" of profane time once again.

A shorter form of *havdalah,* without the use of spices and fire, is recited at the conclusion of major festivals. When a festival falls on Saturday evening, and the conclusion of *Shabbat* does not quite land us in profane time, a special *havdalah* formula is joined to the festival *kiddush.* In this version, we thank God for distinguishing "between holy and holy," referring to the different sorts of holiness borne by festival (*yom tov**) and *Shabbat.*

קַבָּלַת שַׁבָּת
Kabbalat Shabbat

KABBALAT SHABBAT, a special service to welcome the Sabbath (*Shabbat**), has been part of Jewish liturgy for only three and a half centuries. That makes it the most recent major "innovation" in the traditional *siddur**. Created by the mystics in Safed, a town in the Galilee where a great revival of Jewish piety took place in the 16th century, it quickly became a widely accepted and much loved part of Jewish prayer the world over.

The notion of "greeting" the Sabbath as an honored guest was long a well-known part of *Shabbat* lore. So too was the description of this holy day as a "queen." By adding to these the notion of a special Sabbath soul or *neshamah yeterah**, the Kabbalists transformed this welcome into an internal, individual religious act as well as a communal celebration. The chanting of *Kabbalat Shabbat* climaxes in the final verse of the hymn *Lekha Dodi*, a moment when the worshipper is supposed to receive that extra measure of soul. If the prayer is recited before the Sabbath begins, that is also the moment of accepting the obligations of *Shabbat* observance.

The most widely accepted version of *Kabbalat Shabbat* consists of six Psalms, 95–99 and 29, followed by *Lekha Dodi*, composed by Rabbi Shlomo Alkabets of Safed. The service concludes with Psalms 92 (designated in the Bible text as "A Song for the Sabbath Day") and 93, followed by the *'arvit** service.

Hasidic tradition, however, here inserts a profound teaching from the *Zohar*, one that shows how all the worlds join together and evil disappears in this holy moment when the supreme Bride prepares to unite with her Holy Mate.

Kaddish

KADDISH is a public declaration of praise for God. Recited only in the presence of a *minyan**, it calls for the name of God to be praised throughout the world and for the speedy establishment of divine rule over the world. Its central line, recited aloud by the congregation, declares "May His great name be blessed forever and ever!" It is composed in Aramaic, the spoken language of Jews in late antiquity. There are several versions of the *kaddish*, one of which is recited by mourners.

Kaddish originated as a prayer to be recited after a session of *Torah** study. In post-Talmudic times, it was adopted for synagogue use in a wide variety of contexts. Mostly it serves as a doxology, or an often-repeated refrain, within traditional Jewish liturgy. Its primary function is to distinguish between various parts of the service. When a particular section of the liturgy is concluded, a *kaddish* is recited. Thus, in the *Shabbat** morning service, for example, a *kaddish* is recited before *barekhu,* which announces the conclusion of the preparatory Psalms, and the beginning of *shaharit**. Another *kaddish* is placed after the *'amidah**, to indicate the end of *shaharit* and the beginning of the Torah service. After the Torah is returned to the ark (*aron kodesh**), another *kaddish* indicates the beginning of *mussaf**, and so forth. Sometimes a *kaddish* will be inserted to distinguish between two things that should not be confused. This occurs, for instance, with the *kaddish* that immediately follows the reading of the Torah portion, setting it off from the additional *maftir* reading.

The recitation of *kaddish* by mourners is an affirmation that they accept God's rule. It is thus a way of coming to terms with the inevitability of loss and our human inability to prevent death. It affirms that generations will go forward and that God's praises will continue to be heard throughout the world, despite our individual losses. By reciting the *kaddish* aloud the mourner in effect leads the congregation in declaring God's praise and demonstrates that faith helps us to transcend loss. When we stand up in the community and recite *kaddish*, we affirm life itself, even as we face mortality.

קידוש

Kiddush

LITERALLY MEANING "sanctification" or "proclaiming holy," *kiddush* is the special blessing or *berakhah** recited on the Sabbath eve and repeated, in a somewhat different formula, on *Shabbat** morning, usually over a cup of wine. Reciting *kiddush* declares the *Shabbat* holy. From a halakhic (*Halakhah**) point of view, if *kiddush* is recited before sundown on Friday, as it may be, the one who recites it and those who affirm it by responding "Amen" have accepted the Sabbath and are committed to its observance.

The text of the Friday evening *kiddush* describes *Shabbat* as God's loving gift to Israel, given to us in memory of Creation as well as to recall the Exodus from Egypt. This seems to refer to a Sabbath of divine or cosmic dimensions (as partners in Creation, we partake of God's rest after creating the world) that also has a human aspect (we understand, as only liberated slaves can, how much every person deserves and needs rest). Each *Shabbat* is seen as a renewal of both of these moments in our collective memory.

The recitation of *kiddush* is preceded by *va-yekhulu*, Genesis 2:1–3's account of God's rest. Since that account contains thirty-five words, the Sephardic-Hasidic prayer book's text of *kiddush* also has the same number of words (two phrases present in the Ashkenazic text are omitted). Thus, the Sabbath Queen or *shekhinah** "is crowned with seventy crowns," according to the *Zohar*. Each crown is a holy word. Half of these are from the Torah, the word of God above, and half are from the prayer text, the words of Israel below. In the mystical tradition, the *kiddush* over wine culminates the marriagelike celebration of the entire Sabbath eve service.

The daytime *kiddush* is called *kiddusha rabba* ("the great *kiddush*"), perhaps to compensate for its lesser halakhic status. This affirmation of the day's sanctity is briefer, consisting of the simple blessing over wine (or liquor, which may be substituted on this occasion) with an introductory formula. In varying custom, that introduction may be as brief as just the final portion of Exodus 20:11 ("God therefore blessed the Sabbath Day and called it holy"), or may include some combination of the entire Sabbath command of Exodus 20:7–11, Exodus 31:16–17, and the 23rd Psalm.

Kiddush is also recited on major festivals in a formula appropriate to each occasion. While *kiddush* is ordinarily said at the table where the meal is to be eaten, diaspora Ashkenazic custom also has *kiddush* recited in the synagogue. This was originally done for the sake of wayfarers lodging in communal facilities, but eventually it became part of the established rite.

כל נדרי

Kol Nidre

THE EVENING PRAYER on *Yom Kippur** is preceded by *kol nidre,* a legally-worded declaration that nullifies vows to be made in the coming year. The recitation of this formula, one of the best-known portions of all Jewish liturgy, has a long and controversial history. It was already known and debated in the Gaonic period (9th century). The original formula was retroactive, nullifying all vows made in the preceding year. Its recitation would allow one to enter *Yom Kippur* with a clean slate, with no forgotten or unfulfilled vow blocking one's path to atonement. But some argued that the availabilty of such a blanket nullification would encourage people to vow more casually, and then rely on the coming *kol nidre* as an escape from obligation. As a compromise with those who opposed *kol nidre* altogether, the rabbis changed it into an anticipatory rather than a retroactive formula.

The melody used for *kol nidre* is considered to be among the most ancient of the synagogue's repertoire. The recital is an act of high drama. It is preceded by removing two *Torah** scrolls from the ark, held by two elders of the congregation who take the symbolic role of court witnesses. A special formula permitting the congregation "to pray together with the transgressors" is then recited. This formula, which is also in legal language, served in some periods of Jewish history to allow forced apostates to join their Jewish brethren in *Yom Kippur* prayers. That formula, then the *kol nidre* proper, is each recited three times, rising from quiet chant to a great crescendo. The congregation responds by calling out Numbers 15:26: "All the Children of Israel and the strangers in their midst are forgiven, for the whole people has acted unintentionally."

All this must take place before sundown, as release from vows is not permitted on the Sabbath (*Shabbat**). This initial rite of for-giveness concluded, the congregation loudly praises God with the blessing *she-heḥeyanu,* thanks to the One who has "kept us in life, sustained us, and enabled us to reach this time." This blessing, I once heard a wise teacher say, is the very essence of *Yom Kippur.* Here we are—the slate wiped clean once again—ready to stand directly in God's presence with a clear and undivided attention that is possible only on *Yom Kippur.* This blessing is followed directly by the evening service of *Yom Kippur* itself.

כשר, כשרות
Kosher, Kashrut

KASHRUT literally means "fitness," referring in this case to fitness for eating, though the term is also used in many other areas of *Halakhah**. *Kosher* (or *kasher* in the Sephardic and modern Hebrew pronunciation) means "fit" to be eaten or used to prepare food.

The food restrictions of Judaism are based on several originally unrelated Biblical commandments. Leviticus 11 categorizes animals, permitting for food only cud-chewing animals with cloven hooves. Of sea creatures, only those with fins and scales were to be eaten. No defining marks are given for fowl, but there is a list of forbidden birds. The proper method of ritual slaughter, in which blood drains most quickly from the carcass, is based on the prohibition of blood in sacrifices, extended in Deuteronomy 12:20–25 to ordinary slaughter. The prohibition of mixing milk and meat, or meat and dairy-prepared foods altogether, is based on Exodus 23:19, and was probably a Biblical protest against a pagan fertility rite.

The permitting of meat, especially outside a sacrificial context, results from several compromises with what appears to be an originally vegetarian ideal. In Eden and throughout the earliest generations, according to the Bible, Adam and Eve's offspring were natural vegetarians. Only after the flood was meat permitted for human consumption. For Israelites, all meat at first had to be offered to God on the altar. Later the eating of meat was permitted outside the Temple, but with Temple-like restrictions still limiting it, so that those who ate meat would realize that the taking of life is no trivial matter. Vegetarianism as a higher ideal form of *kashrut* has continued to exist among small numbers of Jews and is currently gaining popularity in various Jewish circles.

The Leviticus passage offers "holiness" as the reason or reward for observance of these prohibitions. Various forms of that explanation are widely held throughout the tradition. The Jewish people needs to be kept pure to fulfill its holy mission. *Kashrut* is seen as one of the chief means to such purity, and to keeping the Jews both separate from others and devoted to the word of God. In the life of the individual and family as well, *kashrut* is seen as a discipline that leads to heightened awareness of God's presence, even in such an ordinary and necessary act as eating. "The table is like an altar," say the rabbis, and the way in which food is prepared and consumed should reflect the commitment to a life of holiness.

Along with an increased interest in vegetarianism, new areas of concern that seek to re-define the "fitness for consumption" of certain substances are evolving around the edges of traditional *kashrut*. A halakhic challenge to the use of tobacco has recently been much discussed, based on the principle of "guard your souls (literally: "breaths," but meaning "lives") carefully" (Deuteronomy 4:15). Food and other domestic products produced either by severely oppressed workers or at the cost of serious damage to the environment are also being questioned, as extensions of the principles of *kashrut*.

מנהג

Minhag

A MINHAG or "custom" is a traditionally accepted way of acting, particularly in ritual matters, that is not formally required by religious law (*Halakhah**).

Jewish communities in various parts of the world, while almost universally accepting the authority of Jewish law that had been codified in the Middle Ages, naturally developed their own styles of religious practice. These customs filled in very large areas that are not covered by legislation in the codes: the music to which prayers or Scripture are chanted, foods to be eaten on particular holidays or sacred occasions, the nature of family celebrations of birth, betrothal, and marriage, ways of mourning and memorializing the dead, and a great many more. Some customs were localized to a single *kehillah**, while others spread over large areas and eventually came to embrace most or all of Jewry. Such widespread customs include the *Kabbalat Shabbat** service, *tashlikh* (casting your sins into a body of flowing water) on *Rosh Hashanah**, or the lighting of a *yortseit** candle.

Several leaders of Ashkenazic Jewry in the Middle Ages compiled books of such customs. With the passing of generations, some of these customs found their way into the law codes and became a required part of Jewish practice. Even those that did not become law were taken quite seriously by most religious authorities, following the principle that "the custom of Israel is law." When the early Hasidic masters were persecuted by rabbis and communal leaders in the 18th century, they were primarily accused of violating customs of their community. An old quip notes that the letters of *MiNHaG* are identical to those of *GeHiNoM* or Hell, meaning that Jewish life, if overly dominated by custom, can tend to constrict freedom and stifle religious creativity.

The great changes Jewry has undergone over the last century have very much affected the status of *minhag*. Thousands of Jewish communities have been destroyed or uprooted and their local customs lost. Jewish folklorists have worked avidly to record these before they are entirely forgotten. Non-Orthodox Jews, particularly in North America, have begun to develop their own *minhagim*, some of which have become quite widespread. These include *bat mitzvah**, Confirmation on *Shavu'ot**, and the late Friday evening service. The tendency toward stricter levels of observance within Orthodoxy over the course of recent decades has strengthened the practice of many older *minhagim* and raised them to near halakhic status.

מנחה

Minḥah

MINḤAH is the afternoon service, the second of the three statutory prayer services of each day. It was established as a verbal replacement for the second daily sacrifice in the Temple, offered between sunset and nightfall. While it may be recited as early as midday (half an hour past the solar noon), it is generally done in late afternoon, after more than three-quarters of the day has elapsed.

Minḥah is the briefest of the three services, consisting only of an *'amidah,** preceded by Psalm 145 and followed by the *'alenu* that concludes all services. On *Shabbat** a brief section from the beginning of the following week's *Torah** portion is read.

The word *minḥah* means "gift" or "offering." In the Bible it sometimes refers to the smallest offering—that of flour or grain— permitted those who could not afford an animal sacrifice. The association of the name *minḥah* with this daily service may derive from I Kings 18:36, where Elijah offers a "*minḥah* at evening-time."

Legend has it that Isaac established the *minḥah* service when he "went out to meditate in the field toward evening" (Genesis 24:63). Since Kabbalistic (*Kabbalah**) tradition associates Isaac with *din** or stern judgment (*sefirot**), the fall of evening is seen by the mystics as a time when forces of danger abound. The *minḥah* prayers serve as protection against those forces that will rule from the setting of the sun until midnight, when the anticipation of the coming dawn begins to tilt the balance toward *ḥesed*.

מצוה

Mitsvah

A MITSVAH or "commandment" is a deed in which humans are given an opportunity to fulfill the will of God. That will is inherent within creation itself, as God has created a world that is not yet perfect. The claim of the *mitsvah* is that there is work left for us to do, work that will make us "partners of God in the world's creation," as the *Midrash** says it.

Awareness of *mitsvah* is first manifest in the seven commandments supposedly given to "the Children of Noah." These are incumbent upon all humanity; they comprise the universal moral law as Judaism understands it. The seven Noahide laws are prohibitions against murder, theft, incest/adultery, idolatry, blasphemy, and tearing a limb off a live animal (cruel or wanton destruction of God's creatures). They also include one single positive commandment: to establish courts of justice (i.e., equitable government).

According to the rabbis, Abraham our Father was able to discover and fulfill the divine will before *Torah** was given. A process of deep self-examination allowed him to discover all of the commandments within his own soul. This teaching may be expanded to mean that men and women of exceptional piety, throughout the world, are able to live in such deep harmony with themselves and with nature that God's will becomes clear to them. Religions are attempts to create entire societies that live out the principles seen first by these exceptional individuals.

For the People of Israel, the Sinai revelation expands the number of *mitsvot* to 613, a number nowhere mentioned in the Torah but recorded by the *Talmud** in the name of Rabbi Simlai. These include both positive and negative commandments. They are also divided between *mitsvot* of the devotional ("between person and

God") and ethical/communal ("between person and person")
realms. Since Talmudic times the number of Torah-based commandments has been fixed, but various authors' lists of the 613
show variations. The People of Israel are made holy through
fulfilling the commandments; the *mitsvot* are instruments through
which we dedicate our lives to God. A mystical tradition links the
word *mitsvah* to the Aramaic *be-tsavta* or "together": The *mitsvah* is
the event in which God and the human soul are joined to one
another.

While 613 is the fixed number of *mitsvot* in the Torah, the rabbis
took it upon themselves to add to this number. Such "commandments of the rabbis" (*mitsvot de-rabbanan*) as the lighting of
Hanukkah* candles or the celebration of *Purim** commemorate
events that took place long after the Torah was given. Some
Hasidic authors, commenting on a Talmudic passage that claims
God "multiplied" *mitsvot* for Israel, assert that 613 is much too low
a number. Everything we do in life, they say, should be seen as a
mitsvah, since the soul can be linked to God through every human
deed, and "God needs to be served in every way." This Hasidic
extension of the notion of *mitsvah* may be the source for a broader
understanding of the term in popular Jewish speech, where
mitsvah has come to mean "good deed" or "act of kindness,"
whether or not it is explicitly enjoined by the Torah.

While "everything" may be a *mitsvah* from one point of view,
wholehearted devotion to a single *mitsvah* may have more power to
it than unfeeling commitment to the entire system. *Mitsvot* were
not made to be counted, and no one should be subjected to the test
of "How many *mitsvot* have you performed?" Remember the rabbis'
teaching: "One does more, another does less. The main thing is to
turn your heart toward heaven."

מוסף

Mussaf

THE WORD means "extra" or "additional," and is derived from the root ף-ס-י/y-s-f, "add" or "increase." *Mussaf* is thus related to the name Joseph (*Yosef,* which means "may he increase!"). It refers to the additional *'amidah** recited on Sabbaths (*Shabbat**), Festivals, and New Moons (*Rosh Ḥodesh**), parallel to the additional sacrifices offered on those days in the ancient Temple.

The *mussaf 'amidah* contains seven blessings (expanded to nine on *Rosh Hashanah**), the three introductory and three concluding *berakhot* (*berakhah**) surrounding a single blessing that speaks of the special glories of that day, recalls the Temple, and (in most rites) actually recites the appropriate sacrificial passage from Numbers 28–29.

Cantorial tradition over the centuries has favored the *mussaf* service and embellished it with especially rich musical expression. In some synagogues the cantor typically leads only the Torah and *mussaf* services on *Shabbat.* In Reform and some other liberal congregations, however, *mussaf* has recently been eliminated, abbreviated, or changed due to contemporary discomfort with reciting the details of animal sacrifices.

On *Rosh Hashanah* and *Yom Kippur**, the chief liturgical focus is on this part of the prayer service. On *Rosh Hashanah*, the three sections of Biblical verses declaring God's kingship (*malkhuyot*), memory or providence (*zikhronot*), and power as proclaimed by the *shofar** blast (*shofarot*) are added to the *mussaf 'amidah.* On *Yom Kippur,* the *'avodah* service, which re-enacts the priest's atonement rite in the Temple, is also recited within the *mussaf.*

שחרית

Shaḥarit

SHAḤARIT, the morning worship service, is meant to be recited at dawn, as its name (*shaḥar* = "dawn") indicates. The original intent was that the morning *shema'** be recited before the sun comes over the horizon, and the *'amidah** just at sunrise itself. This timing would make the service correspond to the offering of the dawn sacrifice in the ancient Temple, recognizing the miracle of each day's new dawn and offering a gift in appreciation of it.

Later leniencies have allowed the service, the main one of the day, to be recited at a much later hour, when the powerful moment of witnessing the dawn has long passed. Even when recited later, however, the service still begins with *birkhot ha-shaḥar*, "dawn blessings," acknowledging God's presence in the various stages of rising and dressing in the morning. These blessings are followed by *pesukey de-zimrah*, a group of Psalms intended to arouse devotion in the worshippers and prepare them for prayer.

The *shaḥarit* service itself consists of the recital of the *shema'*, surrounded by three blessings (*berakhah**) and the *'amidah*. On most weekdays the service concludes after the recital of various addenda that follow the *'amidah*. On Mondays and Thursdays, Sabbaths (*Shabbat**), New Moons (*Rosh Ḥodesh**), and Festivals, the *Torah** is brought forth for communal reading before the service is concluded.

שְׁמַע

Shema'

THE SHEMA', or the proclamation "Hear O Israel, the Lord our God, the Lord is One," stands at the center of Jewish worship. The most essential declaration of Jewish faith is learned early in childhood. Pious Jews hope that it will be the last phrase they utter before they die. "His soul went out with the word 'One'" is often found in descriptions of martyrs' deaths.

The *shema'* actually consists of three Biblical passages: Deuteronomy 6:4–9 and 11:13–21 and Numbers 15:37–41. The daily recitation of these passages is considered a Biblically ordained precept ("You shall speak of them . . . when you lie down and when you rise up" [Deuteronomy 6:7]). Although surrounded by prayers, the *shema'* itself is not a prayer. It is addressed to one's fellow Jews, and perhaps also to some broader notion of "Israel" (*yisra'el**). It proclaims God's Oneness, the obligation to love and serve God through the commandments, a warning that satiety due to too much worldly prosperity may lead one to turn away from God, and a faith that righteousness is ultimately rewarded. The *shema'* concludes with an admonition to be holy and to remember that the Lord brought Israel forth from Egypt (*Mitsrayim**) in order to be our God.

It is the first declaration of the *shema'*, however, by which it is best known. The *shema'* is referred to as the proclamation of Divine Oneness. God is One, the Source of all being. There is no demonic realm outside of God, there is no profane or "secular" realm where God's presence cannot be found. God's oneness includes and embraces all; everything exists within God. This interpretation of the *shema'* is perhaps best expressed in the words of a Hasidic master (Rabbi Judah Leib Alter of Ger, 1847–1904, author of *Sefat Emet*):

> The proclamation of oneness that we declare each day in saying "Hear O Israel," and so forth, really needs to be understood as it truly is. That which is entirely clear to me . . . based on the holy writings of great Kabbalists, I am obligated to reveal to you . . . the meaning of "Y–H–W–H* is one" is not that He is the only God, negating other gods (though this too is true!), but the meaning is deeper than that: there is no being other than Him. [This is true] even though it seems otherwise to most people. . . . everything that exists in the world, spiritual and physical, is God Himself. It is only because of the contraction (*tsimtsum**) that was God's will, blessed be He and His name, that holiness descended rung after rung, until actual physical things were formed out of it.
>
> These things are true without a doubt. Because of this, every person can attach himself [to God] wherever he is, through the holiness that exists within every single thing, even corporeal things. You only have to be negated in the spark of holiness. In this way you bring about ascents in the upper worlds, causing true pleasure to God. A person in such a state lacks for nothing, for he can attach himself to God through whatever place he is. This is the foundation of all the mystical formulations in the world.

שבעה

Shiv'ah

SHIV'AH, literally "seven," is the weeklong period of intense mourning following the death of a close relative. The purpose of *shiv'ah* observance, which is usually called "sitting *shiv'ah*," is to allow the mourner time to absorb the shock of loss and to give full expression to grief before returning to the normal routine of work and social obligations.

Shiv'ah begins following the burial service. After returning from the cemetery the mourner is expected to stay at home until the morning of the seventh day. Prayer services, allowing for the recitation of *kaddish** with a *minyan**, are conducted in the mourner's home each morning and evening. Those attending the service and other members of the community are urged to visit and console the mourners. It is considered proper to speak of the deceased and to encourage the mourners to do so as well. While mourners are released from the obligation to study *Torah**, brief study periods, especially study of *Mishnah**, are often arranged before or after prayers in the house of mourning. During *shiv'ah* the mourner is in no way to act as host to his or her comforters. Mourners dress simply, continuing to wear the garment that was cut as a sign of loss at the funeral. Such cosmetic acts as shaving for men or wearing makeup for women are forbidden. The wearing of shoes and sitting on comfortable chairs, both signs of comfort, are also denied to mourners, who originally sat only on the floor (today low stools or hard chairs are usually permitted).

Shiv'ah is suspended on *Shabbat**, when mourners are expected to attend services at the synagogue. If a major festival occurs during the week following a death, *shiv'ah* is eliminated or shortened. The changed circumstances of contemporary life have affected *shiv'ah* practice. It has become common, for example, for mourners to sit *shiv'ah* for part of the week at the home of a deceased parent, then to travel and continue the observance in their own home so that another community or group of friends may have the opportunity to perform the *mitsvah** of *niḥum avelim* or comforting mourners.

תַּעֲנִית

Ta'anit

A TA'ANIT is a day on which neither eating nor drinking is permitted. The only such fast day mentioned in the *Torah** (Leviticus 23:27) is the tenth day of the seventh month or *Yom Kippur.** That fast, lasting from evening to evening, marks the most sacred day on the Hebrew calendar and is the most widely observed fast among Jews the world over.

The traditional calendar also lists five other fast days. Most prominent among these is *Tish'ah be-Av** or the Ninth of Av, commemorating the destruction of both the First and Second Temples. This too is an evening-to-evening fast. The other four, which require fasting only from dawn, are *Tsom Gedaliah*, the 3rd of *Tishrey*, in memory of a popular official slain in ancient Judea; the 10th of *Tevet*, when the Romans besieged Jerusalem; *Ta'anit Esther*, the day preceding *Purim**, following the queen's request (Esther 4:16) that her supporters fast for her; and the 17th of *Tammuz*, when the Roman conquerors breached Jerusalem's wall.

In prior generations, many other public fast days were proclaimed. Some of these were strictly occasional, especially in the course of prayers for rain when the season was delayed, a dangerous and not infrequent occurrence in the Holy Land. Other fast days memorialized various historic tragedies and were observed for centuries, but are now mostly forgotten. These include the twentieth of *Sivan*, a fast to mourn the victims of the Ukrainian massacres in 1648. In recent times public fasts have been proclaimed by various rabbinic bodies, but they are observed only within limited circles.

Private fasting as a means of penitence is also well known in Judaism. Some pious people take on such fasts in three-day regimens, promising to fast on Monday-Thursday-Monday of the coming weeks. Such private fasting is especially practiced in the winter months, during the weeks when the first eight Torah portions of Exodus are read in the synagogue.

In mystical and *mussar** circles, there also exists a practice known as *ta'anit dibbur,* a fast of speaking, whereby the penitent spends a certain number of days in silence.

טהרה/טומאה
Taharah/Tum'ah

TAHARAH is a state of ritual purity, brought about either by careful avoidance of defilement or by observing rites of purification. *Tum'ah* is its opposite, the state of ritual defilement.

The *Torah's** rather complex laws of ritual purity are mostly contained in the Book of Leviticus, also referred to as the Priestly Code. Purity and defilement were originally priestly issues, determining who was fit to serve in the priesthood, to officiate at Temple rites, to partake of sacrificial meals, or to be allowed into the sacred precincts altogether. Along with the specific rules of ritual purity, Leviticus contains numerous admonitions for Israel to be pure, to avoid defilement, and to exist as a holy nation. All of these seem to have been closely related in the eyes of the ancient priesthood.

In its most ancient form, ritual defilement was brought about by physical contact with the mysterious sources of life and death. Blood, semen, childbirth, diseased skin, and corpses are the sources of defilement mentioned in the Torah and for which various ritual remedies are offered. It would seem that the taboo has to do with improper contact with the portals of birth and death, the limits of life as we know it. Those who are in the midst of life are to be protected from its entrance- and exit-ways. If they brush up against these defilements, they need to be "purified" or restored to the world of the properly living. In addition to these categories, Leviticus 11:29–30 offers a list of eight creeping things (moles, mice, and lizards, among others; perhaps once considered deadly) that also bring about ritual impurity.

In current Jewish practice, the *mikveh** or ritual bath is used primarily by women, following their period of menstruation. Use of

the *mikveh* by men (either following an emission or after improper
contact with a menstruant, for example) has become rare except in
Hasidic circles. Handwashing, accompanied by the proper blessing, is considered a lesser form of purification, effective if only the
hands have become defiled. The *tum'ah* arising from contact with
the dead can be removed only by purification through the ashes of
a red heifer, a rite that has not been available since the Second
Temple was destroyed in 70 C.E. Thus all Jews are said to be defiled
in this way, although that defilement has no practical conse-
quences in our day. Pious Jews of priestly descent (*kohen*) maintain the tradition of avoiding contact with the dead by not attending funerals or entering cemeteries.

תְּפִילָה

Tefillah

Tefillah or "prayer" is the living heart of Jewish faith, the daily outpouring of the soul before God. This flow of human emotion may come in the form of joyous exultation or desperate plea. Both are part of the complex and universal phenomenon of prayer. Prayer expresses itself directly in the language the heart knows best. Sometimes it is given expression in words spoken aloud, while at other times prayer is beyond words, the speechless call of the innermost self.

Verbal prayer may be divided into two types: the spontaneous prayer of the moment and the set, prescribed prayer to be recited at a fixed time, or liturgy. The Bible is filled with spontaneous prayers. We need think only of Moses' one-line outcry for the healing of his sister Miriam: "Please Lord, heal her!" (Numbers 12:13), or the many spontaneous prayers of the Psalter (*tehillim**). Miriam too joins the chorus of momentary prayer when she and the women of Israel exult at the sea and cry "Sing to the Lord truly exalted; horse and rider has He cast into the sea" (Exodus 15:21).

Fixed or liturgical prayer also has its roots in the Bible, but it developed much further in post-Biblical Judaism, partly to replace the sacrificial system. Worship was now depicted as the person's gift to God, the human heart being placed on the altar where a token animal had once been offered. "A sacrifice to the Lord is a broken spirit" (Psalm 51:19). The familiar rhythms of fixed prayer serve ideally as a language familiar to the heart, one that can stir it to wakefulness like a friend who comes to remind one of the affections of a silent lover. The words recall God's abiding love and goodness, and we are aroused to respond from our depths. "The Merciful One seeks the heart," the *Talmud** says of prayer. The words are the vehicle to allow this flow from the heart to take place.

Nevertheless, Judaism is quite concerned about the proper forms of prayer. The opening tractate of the *Mishnah** and *Talmud* is *Berakhot,* which deals in great detail with the order, nature, and wording of prayers. The evolution of the *siddur**, in both its traditional and various modern forms, bears witness to the great attention Jews have given to the language of prayer. The tension between this concern for proper form and the full knowledge that true prayer soars far beyond the limits of any language lies close to the heart of true Jewish concern for prayer.

יזכור

Yizkor

YIZKOR or memorial services are conducted four times a year according to widespread Ashkenazic custom. These occasions are *Yom Kippur**, the final days of *Pesah** and *Shavu'ot**, and *Shemini Atseret.**

The word *yizkor* means "May He remember," the opening word of the memorial prayer. Traditionally one recites *yizkor* (referred to as *maskir* in German-Jewish tradition) in memory of close relatives, including parents, siblings, spouse, and children. Many *siddurim* (*siddur**) published in recent years have added prayers for the martyrs of the Holocaust, for Israeli soldiers killed in battle, and for victims of terror attacks against Jews.

The text of the traditional *yizkor* prayer mentions that charity (*tsedakah**) has been given in memory of the deceased. In Jewish folk belief this gift and the recitation of *yizkor* prayers were a way of adding merit to the dead, helping them rise to a higher level of heavenly reward, or at least to be saved from punishment for sins. The belief in *yizkor* was especially strong among Jews of the immigrant generation, many of whom bore great guilt for having forsaken the religious norms of the "old country" and feared their fate in the "other world," in which they still very much continued to believe.

The *yizkor* service traditionally follows directly after the *Torah** and *haftarah** readings on the days mentioned. Some liberal synagogues have moved the *Yom Kippur** *yizkor* service to the afternoon, in order to increase attendance at the concluding services of that day.

חיי הרוח

Spiritual Life

 **אהבה**

Ahavah

AHAVAH means "love." In the religious context it refers to several loves. First is the love of God for Creation and for each individual creature. Because Creation is an eternal process and not just a one-time event, the constant flow of God's love into each creature is the essence of life itself. The one God seeks or chooses to be manifest in an infinite variety of forms; hence the existence of any being indicates that it is affirmed, chosen, loved by the God Who is the Source of all.

Ahavah refers also to the special and mutual love between God and the soul of each human being. We are created in the *tselem elohim** ("Image of God") as soulful beings, each of us bearing the capacity to know God from within by knowing our own soul or *neshamah.** The soul longs to reflect the fullness of divine radiance, to cause God's light to shine forth to the world around it. This is its response in love to the divine love that gives it life.

The special love of God for the Jewish people, the descendants of Abraham, stands within the context of our *berit* or covenant with God. As we committed ourselves at Sinai to serve as a priestly people, channeling God's love to all who seek it, Israel saw itself as especially beloved by God. That love is, on the one hand, unconditional (for God so loved Abraham that his descendants are beloved forever!) and, on the other hand, entirely conditional, dependent upon the job we do as bearers of God's love-message to the world.

From the human point of view, *ahavah* refers to *ahavat ha-shem,* our love for God, which is both commanded and assured. We are also commanded to manifest our love of God through *ahavat ha-beriot,* the love of all people and fellow creatures. Since God is beyond needing our love, that which we can do "for" God begins with the love of others. As Jews we also have an obligation to manifest *ahavat yisra'el,* a special love for our fellow Jews, partners in both spiritual heritage and worldly destiny, a love that transcends all differences of ideology or religious style. *Ahavat Torah,* a love of learning and of involvement with the wisdom of tradition, is also a distinctive feature of love in the spiritual life of Judaism.

'Anavah

'ANAVAH, translated as "humility," or "modesty," is among the highest values of traditional Jewish ethics. It is a value that seems particularly out of favor in our society, where self-promotion and claiming credit are taken for granted as legitimate forms of behavior. Perhaps nowhere more than on this question of humility is there a deep gulf between the values of Judaism (along with most traditional religious cultures) and those of the contemporary Western world.

'Anavah is not a value or an attitude to be practiced only on special occasions or for public display. On the contrary, it is a quality of the heart. Its practice flows naturally from a constant awareness that we are "too small for all the kindness and truth" (Genesis 32:11) that are given us every day. We are unworthy of the constantly renewed gift of life, not because we are particularly bad or sinful, but simply because the gift is so overwhelmingly great.

Our response to this unearned gift and the many that accompany it should be to live simply and without pretense. We should not use wealth, titles, or lists of accomplishments to hide our essential vulnerability. Living the simple life keeps us close to appreciating the basics: life, health, love, friendship, and the beauty of God's Creation. Contact with those less fortunate, especially those facing death, helps to increase our appreciation of life. "Any good that you do," says one *mussar** author, "attribute to God, Who is working within you. The bad that you do you may claim for yourself."

'Anavah means that you seek no credit for goodness, since you take it for granted that such is the way we are to act. Giving to others and helping them is the reason we exist, since it is the only way we can respond to all that has been given to us. To count up and seek credit for the bits of goodness we do is to make God over into a petty merchant, exchanging one-for-one. We should know better.

עבודה

'Avodah

'AVODAH, the term for "worship" in Hebrew, is derived from the root ד-ב-ע/'-b-d, meaning "work," "labor," or "service" as performed by a servant. We are to see ourselves as servants of the Lord (*adonai**), working at God's service.

The teachings of the rabbis in *Pirkey Avot** open with the saying of Simeon the Righteous: "The world is founded upon three things: *Torah**, *'avodah,* and acts of lovingkindness." There *'avodah* refers to sacrifices, as Rabbi Simeon lived while the Temple was yet standing. After its destruction the rabbis made the daring move of calling prayer *'avodah sheba-lev,* the *'avodah* of the heart. This means that the same power of approaching God, whether to show one's love and gratitude or to seek atonement, that had previously lain in the offering of animals, was now transferred to the interior realm. The contrite heart could enter God's presence on its own, without the aid of priest or Temple rite.

The devotional attitude associated with the word *'avodah* is not an easy one for us today. Nothing is more precious to us than our independence, or at least our illusion that we are free to choose the course of our own lives. We are, of course, more free to choose than were previous generations. But *'avodah* demands submission. It calls forth the self that recognizes its own mortality, its own limited ability to forsee and determine its future. From behind our modern veneer this self may still call out: "I am the servant of the blessed Holy One; before God and God's teaching I bow at all times . . ."

The element of labor remains associated with the word *'avodah.* A Hasidic master was asked about the young man who spent all his days in intense and heartfelt prayer. "Shouldn't he *do* something?"

a visitor objected. "Surely he could do some work!" "But don't you see how hard he is working?" replied the *rebbe**. "He's drilling a hole in his heart!" Rabbi Mendel of Kotsk defined what it meant to be a *ḥasid** as "working on oneself."

בטחון

Bitaḥon

*B*ITAḤON means "trust." In a religious context it means trust in God and placing our fate in God's hands. The Psalmist frequently refers to *bitaḥon* as a central part of faith: "Happy is the person who trusts in You" (84:13); "On the day when I fear, I shall trust in You" (56:4); "Trust in the Lord and do good" (37:3). From the Psalms the word has entered the Jewish religious consciousness and it is used almost interchangably with "faith" (*emunah**) in both Hebrew and Yiddish.

Popular conceptions of *bitaḥon* depict a God who will fulfill the desires of those who have sufficient trust. "Trust in God" and you will win that contract, that election, that lottery prize (as long as you remember to buy a ticket!). But more sophisticated religious teachers of all ages have understood that true *bitaḥon* applies only to the long run, not to specifics. *Bitaḥon* means placing your life in God's hands with the understanding that God alone knows what is best for you, for your family, or for this world as a whole. We mortals, never able to see the world with God's eyes, accept our fate as part of that transcendent divine plan.

Jews living today have no easy time with *bitaḥon:* The Holocaust has put such trust to the ultimate test. Many have declared that their trust was betrayed, or was perhaps misguided altogether. No term in the history of the Hebrew language so clearly indicates the recent Jewish shift in values as does *bitaḥon.* In current Israeli usage, *bitaḥon* is "defense," as in *misrad ha-bitaḥon,* "the defense department." Here of course it is earthly rather than heavenly forces in whom "trust" is being placed.

The postmodern religious consciousness, wanting to restore a sacred sense of *bitaḥon* without denying reality, may turn to a

Hasidic reading of Jeremiah 17:7: "Blessed is the person who trusts in the Lord and the Lord is his trust." Why the repetition? Because when we trust in God, all we seek is God's own Self. We trust in God to bring us nothing but God! That trust, one that seeks no reward or vindication other than God's presence, is one that can survive great challenge.

דבקות

Devekut

DEVEKUT is "attachment" or "adherence" to God. A person in a
state of *devekut* has reached a place beyond the ecstasy of worship
(*hitlahavut**) where emotion itself has been transcended and a
deep immersion within the divine Self has taken place. Various
mystics and scholars may discuss whether individual consciousness exists while one is in this state and whether *devekut* consti-
tutes full union of the self with God. The answers to such questions vary from one person and one experience to another and it is
therefore futile to try to resolve them in abstract or absolute ways.
In any case, *devekut* is taken to be the highest goal of Jewish mystical striving.

The verb ד-ב-ק or d–b–k is first used in this connection in several passages in Deuteronomy. "Serve Him and cleave to Him"
(10:20; 13:5); "You who cleave to the Lord God are all alive this
day"(4:4). It is through the commentaries on these verses that later
generations, especially in the mystical tradition, came to develop
and refine this term to describe their own inner experiences.

In Hasidism, a popularized form of Jewish mysticism, the term
devekut is used in a more casual and general way. Each person
should seek to live a life of constant *devekut,* never allowing the
mind to depart from God even for a moment. Techniques for such
constant concentration, inherited from earlier *Kabbalah**,
include meditation on the four-letter name of God (*Y–H–W–H**)
and the mental depicting and unvoiced repetition of those letters
in mantra-like fashion. These techniques are designed to lead us
back to the idealized life of the patriarchs, as described by the great
philosopher Moses Maimonides (1135-1205) in the concluding
chapters of his *Guide to the Perplexed.* The patriarchs, he says,

were able to tend their flocks, maintain their households, and go
about their affairs without ever removing their minds from constant concentration on God. Hasidic teaching seeks to make this
Maimonidean ideal accessible to one and all.

אמונה

Emunah

EMUNAH or "faith" is related to the Hebrew word "Amen." That Biblical response to words of blessing is a statement of support, perhaps best translated as "Be strong!" or "Affirm!" *Emunah* in the Bible thus has the sense of affirmation and trust, a commitment of the entire self to the truth as told, seen, or witnessed. "Israel saw the mighty hand that *Y–H–W–H** had used in Egypt. The people became devoted to *Y–H–W–H* and *trusted* in *Y–H–W–H* and His servant Moses" (Exodus 14:31).

The translation problem here is that the English word "faith" does not have a corresponding verb. One almost needs to reconstruct it to say "and Israel *fayed* in *Y–H–W–H* . . ." The more usual English translation for *le-ha'amin*, the verb form of *emunah*, is "to believe." But "believe" is too intellectual a term. To believe can mean to lend credence to a particular set of propositions. In later philosophical Hebrew, the word is used in just that way. But for the Bible as well as for the early rabbis, *emunah* connotes affirmation with the entire self, affirmation even unto martyrdom. This is more than one would do for mere "belief" in an idea, especially one that is not proven.

The range of meanings conveyed by *emunah* and *le-ha'amin* in Hebrew goes from one of these poles to the other, from intellectual credence to wholehearted trust and dedication. It is perhaps for this reason that the affirmations in the great philosopher Moses Maimonides' (1135-1205) Thirteen Articles of Faith begin each statement with: "I believe with a whole faith . . ." *Belief* in the articles would not suffice without *emunah shlemah*, a faith that carries us far beyond just "believing" into the realm of the greatest sureness.

התבודדות

Hitbodedut

THIS WORD literally means "self-isolation" or separating oneself from the company of others. Historically it has come to mean doing so in order to be alone with God.

The practice of *hitbodedut* is first described in this language by Rabbi Bahya Ibn Pakuda, a philosopher and mystic of the 11th century. He lived in a society where Sufi practice, including meditation, was popular among the Muslim majority. His Judaism reflects the great awe in which he held this practice, one he enthusiastically recommends for his readers.

But if the term is a later one, the practice of solitary prayer and silent standing in God's presence is Biblical in origin. It is widely reflected in the Psalms, in such tales as Abraham's wanderings through the desert and Moses and Elijah's forty days at Horeb, the mountain whose name means "desolation." Jeremiah and others among the prophets also felt the calling to a lonely life of dedication in order to seek God's word. The Biblical practice was continued among later Jewish groups, especially communities such as that at Qumran, the "Dead Sea Scrolls" community, where individual pursuit of God and communal life each had their place.

Practices of *hitbodedut* have varied over the centuries. The followers of Rabbi Abraham Abulafia, from the 13th century onward, had techniques of visualized meditations that they developed with great skill. For them, *hitbodedut* came to mean "concentration" on the images before the inner eye. Some Hasidic leaders continued in this path, especially that of visualizing the letters of prayer.

Others see *hitbodedut* as a time for private, but not necessarily silent, prayer. The followers of Rabbi Naḥman of Bratslav (1772–1810), in fact, insist upon the spoken form. These regular practitioners of *hitbodedut* seek to pray this way for one hour each day, pouring forth spontaneous personal prayer, in whatever language the heart knows best. The purpose of this prayer, they say, is to break the heart, for only in the wholeness of knowing our broken heart can we truly come into God's presence.

Meditation is being revived in our day as a part of Jewish spiritual life. Ancient Jewish techniques are being simplified and updated. Methods of concentration and mindfulness are also being brought into Judaism by those who have learned them elsewhere. All this is for the good, a part of our generation's effort to make the Judaism we hand on to the future richer in this area than it has ever been.

הִתְלַהֲבוּת

Hitlahavut

HITLAHAVUT means "rapture," "enthusiasm," or "ecstasy." It generally refers to a state reached within prayer, though Hasidic masters sometimes report that it can happen outside prayer as well.

The root ל–ה–ב/l–h–v means "flame." *Hitlahavut* means that the soul catches fire and is itself turned into flame. In such moments all obstacles to perceiving God everywhere are consumed in an instant; consciousness and the ecstatic flame are one.

Nowhere in Jewish spiritual literature is *hitlahavut* proclaimed as the *goal* of devotional life. It is a rare and precious moment that happens in the life of those who give themselves wholly to prayer. Usually it comes and goes almost in a flash. But no matter: The real impact of *hitlahavut* is in the *memory* of such moments. They are stored in the contemplative's mind and become important steps on the road toward the much cooler but longer lasting goal of *devekut**, an attachment to God in which one may live and act.

The great masters of Jewish prayer within Hasidism debated the value of ecstasy, and especially of its display in public worship. In circles where religious devotion was taught to be the highest good, it was natural for novices (especially young boys) to "show off" the intensity of their worship and the "heights" of loud and passionate prayer they could reach. Many older and more sophisticated worshippers found such behavior annoying and disturbing to the community at prayer. Others, however, felt a distinction should be made between such childish excesses and true expressions of *hitlahavut*, which should always be welcome in the community and never be deemed a cause of embarrassment.

קדוש, קדושה
Kadosh, Kedushah

"THE BLESSED HOLY ONE," *ha-kadosh, barukh hu*, is the most common designation for God in classic rabbinic sources. It remains a favorite way of referring to God throughout later Jewish speech and writing. *Kadosh* or "holy" is the single attribute that properly belongs to God alone. We can be compassionate based on our own feelings, on identification with the victims of oppression, or because of good training in values. Similarly we may be just, pure, powerful, or good. But we cannot be holy except in relation to God, Who is the only Source of holiness. Judaism sees all possible holiness in the human world as designated by God: Israel, *Shabbat**, the *mishkan** ("tabernacle"), and *Torah** are holy because God has given them and made them holy.

A primary meaning of *kadosh* is "dedicated" or "set aside." When *bet ha-mikdash**, "the Temple," stood and *korbanot* or sacrifices were offered, anything set aside for offering to God was declared *kodesh* (holy). This need and ability to dedicate and make things holy, which is found in all religions, bears witness to our creation in the *tselem elohim** ("image of God").

Kadosh also has about it a sense of loftiness and transcendence; the holiness of God is of a depth that we can never fathom. The best-known Biblical designation of God as "holy" is that of Isaiah 6, where the prophet envisions the angels singing "Holy, holy, holy is the Lord of Hosts; the whole earth is filled with His glory!" When this verse is recited in part of the daily liturgy known as *kedushah*, it is customary to stand on tiptoe and stretch upward three times, as though we were rising to grasp at the unreachable holiness of God. But in daily practice Judaism is also the religion of "You shall be holy, for I the Lord your God am holy" (Leviticus 19:2). This

קל

means that you can indeed become holy by following the ethics of Jewish living: loving your neighbor, protecting the stranger, caring for the poor. God's holiness may indeed be a mystery beyond us, but we realize it in this world by simple and concrete acts of holy living.

Kavvanah

KAVVANAH literally means "direction." In Judaism it refers to *kavvanat ha-lev,* "directing the heart" to God: praying, studying, performing *mitsvot (mitsvah*)* in such a way that we are inwardly turned toward God's presence, offering our words or deeds as gifts upon an inner altar.

The *Talmud** debates in several places the question of whether *mitsvot* require *kavvanah.* Those discussions seem to understand *kavvanah* as intent in a more direct sense. Did one intend, when reading the scroll of Esther, to fulfill the obligation of *Purim*?* Has the starving prisoner, unaware of the calendar, fulfilled the obligation to fast on *Yom Kippur** because he had no food on that day? Generally the rabbis discourage requiring *kavvanah,* since it is so hard to prove or measure. It is safer to judge acts than to claim to know the heart of the actor. When it comes to prayer, however, *kavvanah* is indeed required, because *kavvanah* is the very essence of the act of prayer. Without it there is only the empty recitation of words.

Kabbalah* developed a highly complex system of *kavvanot* or directed meditations around the text of the daily prayers. Each divine name that appeared in the *siddur** was taken as a reference to some permutation of the *sefirot**. The precise wording of the prayer text became the object for seemingly endless commentary and mystical speculation. Praying with the proper *kavvanot* required great amounts of time and patience, in addition to significant Kabbalistic learning.

The early Hasidic masters turned away from the systematic use of *kavvanot,* and returned to a simple notion of *kavvanah* meaning "direction of the heart." An oft-quoted parable in the Hasidic

sources refers to a king who has stored away his precious possessions in a treasure room, locked with a complex set of keys. The
keys were given only to his most special servants, and they too
needed instructions in using them. In our generation the keys have
been lost altogether. All we can do to get to the treasure (and the
King wants us, His beloved children, to have it!) is to smash the
lock. The lock in the parable is the human heart, which is filled
with arrogance and pride. All we can do is break our hearts. When
we come to God in true brokenheartedness, all the locks open on
their own. The truest *kavvanah*, then, is that of the humble heart.

נשמה יתרה
Neshamah Yeterah

NESHAMAH YETERAH is the "extra soul" or extra measure of soul-presence that Jews are said to have on *Shabbat**. This extra soul-presence means that a person feels more attuned to spiritual life on the Sabbath. The intense awareness of divinity that characterizes *Shabbat* observance at its best is caused only partly by the absence of worldly pressures and the vacuum created by withdrawing from them. There is also a positive factor, a divine gift we receive each *Shabbat,* that allows us to live on that different plane. As Sabbath ends, we recognize the departure of the *neshamah yeterah* by smelling spices at *havdalah**: The smell saves us from feeling faint as the extra soul departs. Many Sephardic synagogues have a parallel rite of smelling fragrant green herbs after *Kabbalat Shabbat**, just as the Sabbath begins, to help breathe in the extra soul.

Where does the *neshamah yeterah* dwell on weekdays? Perhaps it is always present within the self, but is able to come forth and express itself only on *Shabbat.* The slowing of our pace, the greater attention paid to the sunset, the open heart of prayer, all convince the extra soul that it may now come forth. The mystical hymn for *Kabbalat Shabbat, Lekha Dodi* ("Come forth, O beloved"), may be understood on one level as a flirtation song between the self and the extra soul, in which the latter is coaxed to emerge from its weekday hiding.

פְּנִימִיּוּת

Penimiyyut

PENIMIYYUT means "inwardness" and is a key value of the religious life, especially as understood by the mussar* and Hasidic (ḥasid*) traditions.

Every person has the potential for an inward life, which stirs both soul and mind. The richness of this life, however, is not to be taken for granted. It must be carefully crafted, the result of study, contemplation, and inner discipline. Penimiyyut is distinguished from ḥitsoniyyut, externality or superficiality. Cultivating the inner life has to begin with a turn (teshuvah*) that leads away from an ordinary understanding of reality toward a deeper perception of the self and the world around us.

Hasidic sources speak of an "inward point" that lies hidden, waiting to be discovered. That point is the presence of God implanted within this world, especially within each person. Our task is to discover that point and to expand it, making it the very center of the way we see both ourselves and others. As we do so, our vision of the world is transformed and we may catch a glimpse of the entire natural order radiant with a supernatural presence that glows from within.

Penimiyyut also reflects the internalization of spiritual gifts and blessings that are described in the Torah* in outward terms. The mishkan* or tabernacle that exists within the heart, the rewards of fertile fields and ample rain, transferred to a heart rich in energy and blessed by the flow of divine bounty, are witness to the transformation of Judaism, especially under Kabbalistic (Kabbalah*) and Hasidic influence, into a religion of penimiyyut.

רוחניות

Ruḥaniyyut

Ruḥaniyyut is "spirituality" in Hebrew. It derives from the word *ruaḥ,* which means both "wind" and "spirit," and was seen by the ancients as a mysterious, Godly wind that blows through the world. The word *ruaḥ* goes back as far as Genesis 1:2: "a wind from God" or "the spirit of God hovered over the face of the waters."

But abstractions like *ruḥaniyyut* are not part of the Biblical way of thinking, and it is no surprise that this word does not appear in Hebrew until the Middle Ages. Part of the Hebrew language's complex history lies in the work of medieval translators. In the 11th and 12th centuries, the great works of Greek and Islamic philosophy, as well as many books of science, were translated into Hebrew, mostly from Arabic. Spanish and North African Jews had read these books in Arabic. But the Jews of Europe now became anxious for this education, and Hebrew, though not spoken, was the only language they read. The problem was that Hebrew, an ancient Semitic tongue, tended toward the concrete and pictorial. It did not have terms for the sorts of abstract concepts that filled the philosophical tracts. The translators remedied this by expanding the Hebrew language, taking ancient roots and finding new ways to create words out of them. *Ruḥaniyyut* (along with its companion *gashmiyyut* or "corporeality") is such a word. It refers to that which contains the presence of God.

The term is most widely used in Hasidism, where it finds its way into Yiddish speech as well. There it is mostly a value statement: A person should devote his or her life to *ruḥaniyyut* (pronounced *rukhniyes* in Yiddish). This refers to such spiritual things as study, prayer, and good deeds, as opposed to *gashmiyyut,* which would mean acquisition of wealth, bodily pleasures, and other "worldly" concerns. While it is true that Judaism is somewhat less other-worldly than this division seems to indicate (note that "good deeds," expressed very concretely, are part of *ruḥaniyyut*), the terms are to be found.

Hasidism struggled mightily with the question of whether true spirituality requires abstinence from the pleasures of this world. On the one hand it may be said that Hasidism was born when the Ba'al Shem Tov (Rabbi Israel ben Eliezer, 1700–1760, the first central figure of Hasidism) rejected asceticism. He realized that God is to be found everywhere, including the ordinary and the physical. Hasidism is characterized by a certain acceptance of worldliness. Yet Hasidism's most profound teachers called for simple living, for finding God's presence in such "ordinary" events as dawn and dusk and in the miracle of life's renewal each day. They viewed "excess" as dangerous to the spiritual life, even in times that could not have conceived the wealth and excess that surround us today.

תשובה

Teshuvah

ONE OF the most important and original terms of Jewish moral thought, *teshuvah* is quite inadequately rendered by the usual translation "repentance." To repent is to turn away from sin and seek forgiveness. *Teshuvah* is a broader concept, one that goes to the very root of human existence. It is no wonder that the *Talmud** lists the power of *teshuvah* as one of those seven things that existed before God created this world. Human life is inconceivable without *teshuvah*.

The first person to undertake *teshuvah* was the very first human. Adam realized the magnitude of his sin in the Garden, according to the *Midrash**, and sought to be reconciled with God. *Teshuvah* in this case would mean re-establishing the intimacy and trust that existed between God and God's beloved creatures before the expulsion from Eden. *Teshuvah,* in this key story, could not mean the re-creation of innocence. That childlike aspect of Eden was gone forever. But a new relationship, one more mature since it had faced and overcome the moment of doubt and betrayal, was Adam's goal. It is this deeper faith, one that emerges from struggle with the self, that is the goal of *teshuvah*.

Another great paradigm of *teshuvah* is the Biblical tale of Jonah. For this reason it is read in the synagogue on *Yom Kippur** afternoon, as the special season of *teshuvah* draws near to its close. God teaches the prophet Jonah not to be cynical, to always maintain faith in the possibility of human transformation, just as God does. The prophet, who had longed for God to destroy the wicked city of Nineveh, is reminded that the city contains "more than a hundred and twenty thousand people who do not know their right hand from their left, and much cattle" (Jonah 4:11). Most sinners are like fools or children, not knowing right from left, no more guilty than cattle. Their Creator does not want to destroy them, but to see them transform their lives by turning to God.

The *Kabbalah** views *teshuvah* as a cosmic process, one that extends beyond humans and encompasses all life and being. It is identified with *binah*, the third of the ten *sefirot** and the maternal force within God. All creatures are derived from the divine womb, and all contain within them a deep longing to return to that source. The human desire to reach out to God is as whole and natural as the tree's stretching to grow toward the sunlight or the root's sinking deeper into the earth in quest for water.

יֵצֶר הַטוֹב
יֵצֶר הָרָע

Yetser ha-Tov
Yetser ha-Ra'

THE "GOOD AND EVIL INCLINATIONS" are the forces within each person that lead us to do good and evil, according to the psychology of the early rabbis. Sometimes these forces are personified and depicted as quarreling with one another inside us, each arguing that we should follow its path.

The *Torah** speaks only of the evil inclination, in passages (Genesis 6:5; 8:21) where God sadly concludes that the creation of humans was regrettable since their inclinations turn only to evil. The rabbinic tradition, apparently unwilling to affirm the pessimism of these passages, created a parallel "good urge," with the human soul a *tabula rasa* upon which the forces of good and evil fight out their battles. For the Kabbalists (*Kabbalah**), who believe there are demonic forces in the universe that threaten the Divine Presence, the good and evil urges become the internalized representations of these mighty forces that act on the cosmic as well as the personal scale.

An alternative psychology to that of good and evil inclinations is found in the midrashic and mystical notions of *kelipah** and *pri* or "shell" and "fruit." Here the mind or soul is compared to a delicate fruit that needs to develop a hard shell around itself for protection. The truest self lies within. This is the "fruit," not subject to evil or corruption. But the *kelipah,* which was originally seen as a protective device, may turn evil or even demonic and keep the inner self from expression. Here the psychological model is that of the good inner self seeking to escape (yet still needing) its shell, rather than the neutral self before the two warring forces.

יראה

Yir'ah

YIR'AH is "fear," referring to *yir'at ha-shem*, "the fear of the Lord." "What does the Lord God want of you except that you fear the Lord your God, walk in His ways and love Him, serving the Lord your God with all your heart and soul?" (Deuteronomy 10:12). This statement appears shortly after this passage: "You shall love the Lord your God with all your heart, with all your soul, and with all your might" (Deuteronomy 6:5). Judaism has always insisted on the proper balance of love and fear as ideal for maintaining the religious life.

But what does it mean "to fear the Lord?" Is it to be taken literally: to be *afraid* of God? What is it that I should fear in God? That He might take my life away? Then it is death, rather than God, that I fear. Or will He make me suffer? Then it is suffering I fear. That He might punish me for my sins? My guilt is speaking through me, and it is the pain of punishment and of facing myself, more than the Lord, that I fear. Jewish ethicists through the ages have debated whether these lower levels of *yir'ah* are of any value at all. Certainly they are not what these thinkers have in mind when speaking of *yir'ah* in a positive sense.

But suppose that punishment for sin consists of God being far from me, of my feeling no closeness to the One I love? Then *yir'ah* exists in counterpoint to *ahavah**, the love of God. It is precisely because I love God that I fear doing that which will trangress God's intent for me. *Yir'ah* here becomes a longing to do only what God desires. Many authors praise such *yir'ah*. But if taken too far it can also lead to a religion of anxiety. *Shalom** is hardly possible if I am constantly pursued by the inadequacy of my religious life, by a fear that I am not yet doing what God wants.

Another understanding of *yir'ah* associates it with awe, a great sense of trembling before the greatness of God. Here we think of the *Torah's** description of Mount Sinai: "All the people, seeing the thunderbolts and torches and hearing the *shofar** sounding as the mountain smoked—the people were frightened; they trembled and stood far off" (Exodus 20:14). Awe causes us to distance ourselves from God, not to become overly familiar, to take God's presence for granted. But this *yir'ah* also exists in balance with love. If the love of God brings me close to the One, what place is there for awe and distance? This paradox is answered by a well-known mystical reading of the Song of Songs: "His left hand is beneath my head, while His right hand embraces me" (2:6). The left hand of God, representing *din**, seems to insist on *yir'ah*, to demand a distance between God and the soul. But even as that left hand of God pushes me away, I know that God also embraces me to draw me near. This too is part of the mystery of faith.

יסורים

Yissurim

YISSURIM is "suffering." In a religious context it may refer to several sorts of suffering, some physical and some existential. The figure of the righteous one (*tsaddik**) who suffers is well known in Judaism, not only as a theological conundrum but as a symbol of Jewish existence through history. This image of Israel as the righteous suffering servant of God, first created by the second prophet who wrote under the name of Isaiah, has been central to the way Jews have seen their fate for more than two millennia. Of course there have been significant periods when the picture was largely an accurate one, thanks to the nations in whose midst and at whose whim we lived. But recent history also shows that even when this is by no means our situation, it is hard for us to break loose from the ancient and deeply rooted pattern.

The classic example of suffering in Judaism is surprisingly not that of Job, but of the generation of the Bar Kokhba rebellion (132–135 C.E.), known in classical Hebrew as *doro shel shmad,* the generation of destruction. The tearful recounting of the deaths of the ten martyrs of those times has been a part of the Ashkenazic *Yom Kippur** service for many centuries. Rabbi Akiva, the best-known figure of that group, is Judaism's classic martyr. Akiva spoke of his sufferings as *yissurim shel ahavah,* sufferings of love. He thus bequeathed to future generations a rich and complex lens of self-understanding.

Sufferings of love may mean that we who love God continue to do so, despite our suffering. We may go farther, using our suffering itself as a way of loving God, offering ourselves, as it were, on the altar of suffering and transforming that suffering into a gift to God. Such a love of God is difficult, but it can lead to a more mature and less fantasy-dependent faith. This offering may be of physical pain due to illness or injury, or the pain of loneliness and loss due to the deaths of those we love. But the pains of doubt and lack of spiritual direction are also part of *yissurim,* and these are still harder to give as gifts to a God about whom we might be confused or uncertain.

But "sufferings of love" has another dimension as well, rooted in the wisdom traditions of the Bible: "God reproves the one He loves" (Proverbs 3:12); "Blessed is the man whom God causes to suffer, teaching him from His *Torah**" (Psalm 94:12). Here we get the sense that the love may be God's, and that God brings suffering to us as a gift, knowing that it will bring us to a truer or deeper faith. Learning to accept suffering as a gift from the One who loves us is the task of a lifetime, and perhaps more.

זכות

Zekhut

ZEKHUT is usually translated "merit." In the heavenly balancing of good and evil deeds, it is the "credit" we receive on the side of the good. This *zekhut* may be because of an entire life of piety or because of some single half-forgotten good deed done long ago. It may be the result of *tsedakah** given in our own name or could derive from the great merit of an ancestor or relative. It may simply be part of the *zekhut* that belongs to all Jews because we are descendants of the *avot**, whose store of divine blessing is never exhausted.

Zekhut is also used in the sense of a special privilege we are rarely given. This might be the privilege of meeting or hearing a wise or great person, or the rare opportunity to perform the sort of *mitsvah** or an act of *tikkun 'olam** that few of us have the chance to fulfill. In such moments, we might be tempted to say the words of the students of Rabbi Simeon ben Yohai, after he has taught them some profound secret of *Kabbalah**: "Blessed are we. Had we come into the world only for this moment, it would have been sufficient."

חיי הכלל

Community,
Life with Others

Avot

THE AVOT or "forefathers" in Judaism are the three patriarchs—Abraham, Isaac, and Jacob. Though other Biblical characters are venerated in many ways, only these three are called *avot*.

The *Torah** tells of God's love for the *avot* and their faithfulness to God's covenant. In faithfulness to them, God has brought their descendants, the People of Israel, forth from Egypt. The Exodus extends to the entire people the special bond that had existed between God and their first ancestors. Throughout Jewish history, we have seen ourselves as redeemed by the merits of our ancestors. In this context, the word *avot* is sometimes extended to refer to the righteous of all prior ages.

The *Midrash** describes Abraham as a seeker after God, one who tried out various forms of religion until he arrived at his true faith. The Torah itself rather sees God as the seeker, looking for a righteous human being in a sinful world. God finds in Abraham the one person who might best propagate the divine message. While the Bible mentions Abraham's faith (Genesis 15:6), the rabbis find Biblical "evidence" (Genesis 26:5) to insist that Abraham was fully observant of the commandments long before they were given to Moses. He knew them all by turning inward, because every human being contains the entire Torah. The *Kabbalah** sees Abraham as standing for divine love. "The attribute of love said before the blessed Holy One: 'As long as Abraham our Father was in the world, I had nothing to do, because he stood my guard.'"

Isaac, about whom Scripture has much less to say, is associated by Kabbalistic tradition with *yir'ah**, the fear of God. While bound to the altar on Mount Moriah, where Abraham had taken him to be sacrificed, the *Midrash* says, Isaac was looking upward, and he saw more than human beings in this life are fit to see. The angels wept at father and son's devotion to God, but their hot tears fell into Isaac's eyes and blinded him. Indeed, the next major Biblical tale that involves Isaac depicts him as elderly and blind. Such a patriarch, survivor of a divine encounter that terrified him, teaches us the fear of God.

Jacob is the morally problematic patriarch in the Biblical text. He tricks his brother Esau out of both birthright and blessing, and then tricks Laban into giving him a large—and perhaps well-deserved—part of his flock. But the later Jewish tradition sees his actions as entirely justified and treats Jacob as "the choicest among the patriarchs." He is called "a man who bore the beauty of Adam," the one person "whose image is engraved on the throne of glory." Perhaps these extreme formulations are overcompensating. Realizing and accepting the trickster element in Jacob's personality is hard for Jewish readers, whose enemies have often accused them of being overly clever to the point of cunning. We prefer to see Jacob as the one who dreams of ladders reaching to heaven, or the ancestor who struggles with angels (*Yisra'el**). We celebrate his great love for his beloved Rachel and her children and feel with him in his tragic fatherhood when he mourns for Joseph. For the Kabbalists, Jacob represents compassion or peace, since he brings into harmony and balance the conflicting legacies—love and fear—of his grandfather and father.

דרך ארץ
Derekh Erets

LITERALLY MEANING "the way of the world," *derekh erets* is a rich complex of values and ideas that are used in a variety of contexts.

On what might be its most superficial plane, *derekh erets* refers to good manners, the "proper" way to behave. The term seems to mean that these things are to be taken for granted by anyone and need·not be specifically prescribed by the *Torah**. Related to this meaning is *derekh erets* as proper respect for those generally thought to deserve it—parents, teachers, elders, the learned, and those in authority. When the *Talmud** says that "*derekh erets* preceded Torah," it partly means that such norms of respect are held by non-Jews as well, and are basic to all of human civilization.

But *derekh erets* also has a sexual meaning; it is "the way of the world" as in fulfilling one's natural instincts. This too preceded Torah; in fact, some laws of Torah are seen as a response to such *derekh erets*, a taming of instinctive behavior. We share sexual desire and the reproductive process with the animal kingdom, but our task is to put these into the context of relationship and holiness (*kedushah**).

Perhaps the oldest meaning of *derekh erets* connects it to death, "the way of all the earth" (Joshua 23:14). The folk wisdom or "manners" of *derekh erets* are then those we learn from the primary lesson of mortality: the conduct of a person who knows he or she is going to die. All of these meanings are occasionally seen as interconnected in subtle and interesting ways.

חסיד

Ḥasid

A ḤASID is a devotee, an enthusiastic follower or worshipper. Ḥasid is derived from ḥesed, a free-flowing love that knows no bounds. A ḥasid is one who will give of him- or herself entirely.

Special Jewish devotional groups have been called ḥasidim throughout the ages. The *Mishnah** refers to "ḥasidim of early times." *Pirkey Avot** describes a ḥasid as one who says: "What's yours is yours and what's mine is yours," one who is generous without a thought of self. The same source warns, however, that "an ignorant person is no ḥasid." Typically of Judaism, a measure of learning needs to be added to the simple joy of giving that is the ḥasid's lot.

Those who are called ḥasidim today mostly stem from the great revival movement called Hasidism that began in Eastern Europe in the mid-18th century. Its first central figure was Rabbi Israel ben Eliezer Ba'al Shem Tov (literally: "master of the good name"), who lived from 1700 to 1760. The BeSHT, an acronym by which he is often called, was a charismatic mystic who experienced "soul ascents" into the upper worlds ('olam*) and who had great insight into the souls of those around him. He taught a Judaism based on love (of God, of *Torah**, and of fellow Jews) and warned against excessive guilt over sins or attempts to punish the body. Simplicity, joy, and wholeness in worship were the key themes in the immensely successful religious movement that emerged in the decades following his death.

Hasidism has existed as a complex historical phenomenon over the past two hundred and fifty years. Originally condemned by the rabbinate as radically innovative and dangerous, it came to be accepted by the establishment in the early 19th century.

As other Eastern European Jews abandoned tradition for modernity in various forms, the faithful *ḥasidim* were identified with ultra-Orthodoxy. The surviving Hasidic communities today, primarily in Israel and the United States, exist as a result of nearly superhuman efforts to rebuild a way of life completely shattered by the Holocaust.

Since the early 20th century, many Jewish writers and thinkers have tried to teach the values of Hasidism to Jews (and non-Jews) who live outside the Hasidic community and its traditional way of life. They believe that the key message of Hasidism—that each person can become aware of God's presence throughout the world and should live each moment as though standing in that presence—needs to be made available to everyone. This approach, sometimes termed neo-Hasidism, is very much shunned by the *ḥasidim* themselves, who take complete loyalty to traditional Jewish life as the very basis of Hasidism. Nevertheless, neo-Hasidism has had considerable impact on the general Jewish community through its teachings, its joyous, fervent music, and its revised hierarchy of religious values.

חבורה

Ḥavurah

Ḥavurah is related to the word *ḥaver*, "friend," and to *ḥibbur*, "joining." A *ḥavurah* is a group of friends joined together for the purpose of spiritual quest, a search for Jewish growth and learning, or shared celebration of the Jewish year and its members' Jewish lives. Our *ḥavurah* is our religious community, the group of people with whom we can share our souls' strivings, celebrations, doubts, and longings.

Ḥavurot or small, intentional religious communities have existed throughout Jewish history in differing forms and under various names. The "band of prophets" (I Samuel 10:5) may have been such a group in Biblical times. The Dead Sea Scrolls speak of a *yaḥad*, which probably means community or sect, who agreed to follow a monastic rule. The Pharisees, a few generations later, developed *ḥavurot* (this is where the term first appears) whose members took special care in observing rules of personal purity that were being extended from priests and levites into small circles of "lay" devotees.

Mystical teachings in Judaism have a special connection to the notion of *ḥavurah*. Because mystical interpretations of texts were considered esoteric and potentially dangerous, they were restricted to closed circles of the initiated. This was true of those who "went down to the divine chariot," the visionary mystics of late antiquity, as well as the *ḥasidim* (*ḥasid**) of medieval Germany and later circles of mystics in Spain, *Erets Yisra'el**, and elsewhere. Only in East European Hasidism, an intentionally popularizing movement, was access to those activities made available to a broader public. Even in Hasidism, however, much of the most significant spiritual activity takes place within what could be called *ḥavurot*, small groups of the most intimate disciples who gathered around their *rebbe**.

The notion of *havurah* has been revived in American Jewish life since the late 1960s. This revival is partly a reaction against the large, somewhat impersonal, modern American synagogue and its highly formalized style of worship. It is also a Jewish version of the American counterculture's interest in old/new spiritual forms and the re-creation of communities that allow for intimacy and deep communication. The new *havurah* is partly an attempt to bring to Jews outside ultra-Orthodoxy the same strong commitment, spiritual intensity, personal bonding, and warm informality that have characterized the Hasidic community and *shtibl* ("prayer house") at their best. The past several decades have seen great influence of *havurot*, their members, and their values on many aspects of Jewish life. In some cases *havurot* also become surrogate extended families for their members, in an age where frequent moving and differences in religious practice keep the biological extended family from serving as the locus of a home and family-based Judaism.

אמהות

Imahot

THE FOUR MATRIARCHS (*imahot*) of the Jewish people are Sarah, Rebekkah, Leah, and Rachel. Long neglected by the mostly male-centered religious language of Judaism, the *imahot* have been reclaimed as role models and symbolic figures by recent generations of Jewish women. A great variety of qualities has been attributed to them through careful readings and re-interpretations of the Biblical tales in which they figure.

Devotion to the *imahot* is not entirely new, however. They are often referred to in such Jewish women's literature as the *Tsena Urena,* a Yiddish paraphrase of the Bible popular in Eastern Europe, and the *tehinot**. The grave of Rachel in Bethlehem (Genesis 35:19; the other three *imahot* are buried in the Cave of Machpelah in Hebron, along with their husbands) is a place of special women's devotion. Women often go to pray there in connection with problems of fertility, identifying with Mother Rachel, whose own womb was closed in the earlier years of her marriage. Such pilgrimages are an especially strong part of women's religious culture in some Sephardic communities.

Recent feminist inquiry has sought to add other important female figures of ancient Jewish memory to the list of *imahot*. Such Biblical figures as Miriam, Deborah, Ruth, and Esther immediately come to mind. Some circles are also attempting to "rehabilitate" the memories of women whom Scripture seems to treat unfairly, because the tales about them were written from a male point of view. Eve, Hagar, and Vashti are among those most discussed in this context.

קהילה

Kehillah

KEHILLAH, a gathering of people, is translated as "community" or "congregation," depending upon the context. In traditional sources it generally refers to an entire Jewish community, to all the Jews living in a particular location. This is the body to which, in pre-modern times, individual Jews owed their primary allegiance. The *kehillah* maintained courts, schools, synagogues, bathhouses (*mikveh**), hospices for the poor and for wayfarers, and other institutions required for Jewish life. Jews paid taxes to the *kehillah*, which in many cases also served as the conduit for tax money to the secular authorities. The responsibilities of *kehillah* membership were incumbent upon all Jewish householders. Leadership positions, including rabbinical appointments, were usually chosen by a small group of wealthy, learned, or otherwise prominent *kehillah* members.

Modern times are characterized by the breakup of this traditional *kehillah* structure. Once Jews were welcomed as citizens of the various countries in which they lived, the function of the *kehillah* as intermediary between the Jew and the state became an anachronism. Without this role, the civil authorities had no interest in enforcing *kehillah* membership, which then became more or less voluntary. At about the same time (mid–19th century), the beginnings of religious reform also led to the splitting of the *kehillah* or Jewish community into various factions or congregations. Thus the meaning of the term shifts from characterizing the Jewish community as a whole to denoting the membership of a particular synagogue.

In a time when the unity of the Jewish people seems threatened, perhaps we should reconsider some sort of unified *kehillah* system.

For payment of a nominal fee one could be a member of the Jewish community. This membership might entitle one to receive community bulletins and invitations to community-wide events. Membership would be strictly voluntary, with the understanding that acceptance of *kehillah* dues does not qualify one halakhically as a Jew, a matter that is left to rabbis of the respective denominations.

קידוש השם
חילול השם

Kiddush ha-Shem
Ḥillul ha-Shem

THE "SANCTIFICATION" and "profanation" of God's name are of great concern in the value system of traditional Jewry. *Kiddush ha-shem* is a public witnessing of Jewish faith, an act that brings glory to God and honor to the witness. It may take the drastic form of martyrdom, and the term is historically often associated with that act. But *kiddush ha-shem* may take many lesser forms as well. An identified Jew who risks his or her own life for the sake of others may be said to have performed a *kiddush ha-shem*, an act that raises the public moral image of Judaism. A deed of unusual generosity or kindness far beyond what the law requires, once it becomes public, may also be seen as a *kiddush ha-shem*.

Conversely, a *ḥillul ha-shem* or a desecration of God's name is that which brings Judaism into ill repute. A newspaper report that a well-known pious Jew is a slumlord or has been caught profiting illegally from nursing homes where the elderly are poorly treated is shudderingly discussed in the community as a *ḥillul ha-shem*. Such a Jew has not only violated the *Torah** and been disgraced personally. The reputation of Jewish piety has also been harmed. It is as though the good name of God has been tarnished by one who is seen as a worshipper and now revealed as a hypocrite. In a world where religious Jews are a minority within a minority, such an offense needs to be treated most seriously.

משיח

Mashiaḥ

THE WORD *mashiaḥ* or messiah literally means "anointed one." It is used in the Bible to refer to both priests and kings who were anointed. Since Second Temple times (the later prophecies in the Book of Isaiah, c. 400 B.C.E.) it refers to an appointed redeemer, a descendant of the royal house of David, who will appear at the end of time to deliver Israel from exile and rule over a godly kingdom on earth that will be centered in Jerusalem and will embrace the righteous of all nations.

Many versions of this widespread and popular belief are preserved in ancient Jewish sources. Some saw the messiah in rather naturalistic terms, as a righteous and powerful human ruler who would bring an end to all oppression. Others depicted a more supernatural figure, one who would conquer his foes by the word of God alone, and in whose day nature itself would be transformed, offering a life of endless bounty to the living. The dead would be resurrected and live again on earth. According to some sources, the messiah has in fact existed since the beginning of time and only awaits God's word as to when he will be allowed to reveal himself. (The idea of a messiah who is not a "he" has not been entertained until very recent times!)

Messianic movements have existed in Judaism throughout its history. Christianity may to some degree be seen as the earliest and most successful of these movements, and one that had tremendous influence on all of later Judaism. For those Jews who were not convinced by the Christian messianic claim, however, the spirit of potential messianism was by no means diminished. In every century of Jewish history there have been messianic claimants. The best-known of these is the 17th-century Turkish Jew Shabbatai

Tsvi, whose messiahship was supported by many of the leading rabbis of his day. In very recent times there has been a significant messianic outburst among Hasidic Jews of the Lubavitch sect, who have claimed that their late leader, Rabbi Menahem M. Schneersohn, is the messiah. Like all messianic claims, this has led to great conflict within the Jewish community.

Perhaps the most interesting aspect of Jewish messianism is its secularization. The claim has often been made that modern Jews who lost much of their faith in God did not as easily lose their faith in messianic redemption. The various movements for social progress that have attracted so many Jews, including Socialism and Communism, may be seen as forms of secular messianism. The same is true of Zionism. While viewed as countermessianic by the ultra-Orthodox, who preferred to wait for God's anointed before returning to the Holy Land, the Zionists set about doing one aspect of messiah's work: ending the historical exile of Jewry. In that sense Theodor Herzl, the founder of political Zionism, may be seen as the second great success among messianic figures in Jewish history—although neither one has yet brought about the world's redemption.

מנין

Minyan

A MINYAN is a group or "quorum" of ten adult Jews who collectively constitute a "public" setting. The word minyan literally means "count." A religious act performed in an assembly of ten or more is considered a public act. Since rabbinic tradition values community, public prayer is considered to be of higher merit than private prayer. To pray with a minyan every day is thus an important value. Certain portions of the liturgy, notably barekhu (the call to worship), kedushah (kadosh*) (with its responsive format), and all recitations of the kaddish* require a minyan. Reading from the Torah* scroll and the entire liturgy of taking out the Torah from the ark and returning it are also eliminated from the worship service if there is no minyan.

Other religious events that require a minyan—if at all possible—are circumcisions, weddings, and burials. None of these is to be delayed beyond its proper time, however, if a minyan cannot be gathered.

Traditionally, adult males from the age of bar mitsvah* are counted in a minyan. Tradition allows that a boy close to bar mitsvah, if holding a Torah scroll, may be counted as a tenth member of the minyan if none other is available. Over the past three decades, nearly all Jews outside of Orthodoxy have begun to include women in the count for a minyan. This innovation has caused considerable controversy within the Conservative movement, but the forces for change seem to have won the day.

Minyan is also a name given to a group of Jews (of any size above ten) who meet regularly for prayer. A minyan usually does not have a synagogue of its own, but meets in borrowed or rented space. Such informal prayer groups exist within both the Orthodox and non-Orthodox communities.

מוסר

Mussar

Mussar is the Hebrew term for "ethics" or ethical teachings. Based on the word's origins, it might also be translated "self-discipline" or "moral restraint." The verb ר–ס–י/y–s–r, from which it derives, is often used in the Book of Proverbs meaning "to discipline," but with a tone of threatened punishment behind it.

Jewish *mussar* teachings actually combine religious philosophy, psychology of religion, devotional preaching, and ethics. The long tradition of such writings is said by some to begin with *The Duties of Hearts,* written in Arabic in 11th-century Spain by Bahya Ibn Pakuda. Other classics of the *mussar* tradition include *The Beginning of Wisdom* by Elijah Da Vidas (Safed, 16th century, much influenced by *Kabbalah**); *The True Measure* by Zevi Hirsch Koidenover (Poland, 17th century); and *The Path of the Upright* by Moshe Hayyim Luzzatto (Italy, 18th century). These works enjoyed great popularity among Jews for many centuries and were frequently reprinted, both in Hebrew and in Yiddish or Ladino translations.

In the latter half of the 19th century, an ethics-based revivalist movement took place within the *yeshivah** communities of Lithuania and Byelorussia, areas that were not dominated by Hasidism. In these circles, the enthusiasm (*hitlahavut**) of Hasidism was both derided and imitated, though with special emphasis on ethical self-purification and examination of conscience. The *mussar* classics, especially the work by Luzzatto, were studied intensively with an eye toward constant personal self-improvement. In some cases students were assigned a *mussar* partner, one with whom you studied these works but to whom you could also confess your own moral failings and areas of weakness. Although in theory *mussar* circles did not share Hasidism's belief in charismatic religious leadership, the glorification of certain teachers as outstanding examples of ethical piety has tended in more recent times to offer a "Lithuanian"-style version of the Hasidic master, a sage in whose wisdom followers place their complete trust.

Navi

A *NAVI* or "prophet" claims to bear God's word within him- or herself (*nevi'ah* is the feminine form) and speak in God's name. Some *nevi'im,* like Moses, Elijah, and Elisha, are known through narrative portions of the *tanakh*,* and various miraculous tales are associated with them. Others, including Isaiah, Amos, and most of the other "latter prophets" of the Bible, are known only through their collected prophecies. In most cases rather little of their personal lives is recorded.

The relationship between the prophet's own mind, education, and creative impulse, and the prophecy "given" has long been thrashed out by commentators. There have always been literalists, who believe the prophet to be merely a passive instrument into whose mouth God places the very words he or she is to speak. Others have long held the prophet to be an active participant in the process of revelation. Filled and consumed by the divine message, prophets put it into words using their own powers of articulation and the tools of the literary/religious tradition in which they stand.

The rabbis insisted that prophecy had ceased when the Second Temple was destroyed. This was required to legitimate their own undertaking: the interpretation of an already closed canon of sacred books. They came to assert that "a sage is better than a prophet." Actually the latest prophetic book to enter the Biblical canon is probably Malachai, written in early Second Temple times. By the 2nd century B.C.E., the phenomenon that had once made for prophecy had shifted into the apocalyptic mode, revealing great "secrets" about the future and warning repeatedly of the great cataclysm to come. These writings were often hidden under the cloak of attribution to the ancients, bringing forth such titles as "The

Testament of Abraham" or "The Visions of Enoch." The rabbis explicitly called these works "extraneous books" and refused to include them in the canon.

Postbiblical Judaism lives beyond the reach of current prophecy. God is still present and accessible in daily life and may be addressed through prayer. But God no longer speaks as happened in prophetic times. Divine silence is a mystery that we have learned to accept, despite an occasional outcry of protest. We study the prophets of old, endlessly re-interpret their words, and still feel morally challenged by them. We produce poets and writers who occasionally don the prophetic mantle, but we are as cautious of them as we are moved by their efforts. In the messianic future, whenever and whatever it will be, we are told that true prophecy will be reborn. Meanwhile, we can only live and witness the mystery of God's silence.

Rav

RAV means "rabbi," one who has been ordained by proper authorities to teach *Torah** and to issue rulings on matters of *halakhah**. Traditionally, Jews turn to a *rav* with questions concerning matters of religious practice and are obliged to follow the decisions received, which are based on the *rav's* careful study of sources. Only certain *rabbanim* (plural of *rav*) are permitted to respond on civil matters and to serve on rabbinic courts that may be convened to adjudicate monetary disputes.

The modern rabbi (also referred to as *rav* in Hebrew; some authorities use *rav* also for female rabbis, while others insist on the feminine *rabbah*) is rather different from this traditional picture in both training and function. The rabbi is seen today as spiritual leader, educator, personal model, and (all too often, especially in small communities) administrator of a Jewish community (*kehillah**). He or she (all forms of Judaism outside Orthodoxy accept women as rabbis) is usually trained in a seminary rather than a *yeshivah**. Noninstitutional ordination by individual rabbis, a traditional path that has always existed within Orthodoxy, has also been revived in some non-Orthodox circles. Rather than studying only *Talmud** and legal codes, today's rabbi will be trained in Hebrew language, Bible, Jewish thought, history, literature, and a wide range of pastoral, interpersonal, and administrative skills. Some rabbis train for and develop specialized rabbinic careers: the rabbi-educator, the rabbi-youth worker, the rabbi-geriatric specialist, and so forth.

The *rav* is still present in the modern rabbi insofar as the rabbinic career is based on learning, commitment to the preservation of the Jewish people and its traditions, and the courage to act decisively, even sometimes at great personal risk, as a moral leader.

רבּי

Rebbe

REBBE is the Eastern European pronunciation of the word "rabbi," formed by adding the possessive ending to the word *rav*, meaning "my teacher." It is the form of address used for a teacher in the *yeshivah** setting.

In the context of Hasidism (*ḥasid**), the term *rebbe* takes on a different meaning. Here it refers to the head of a Hasidic group or following. A *rebbe* is leader and teacher of his *ḥasidim* by virtue of exemplary piety, of learning that exhibits a particularly spiritual tone, and of descent or discipleship that places him in the lineage of Rabbi Israel Ba'al Shem Tov (1700–1760), Hasidism's original charismatic leader.

In the earliest generation of Hasidism, discipleship rather than family heritage made one a *rebbe*. The circles around the Ba'al Shem Tov, his successor Rabbi Dov Baer of Mezritch (died 1772), and their various followers included young men of quite varied backgrounds. Many came from fine families but had rebelled against their fathers or fathers-in-law in seeking out these controversial teachers of mystic lore and spiritual wakefulness. Several of these original Hasidic masters seem to have shared the special charismatic gifts of the Ba'al Shem Tov. By its third generation, however, Hasidic leadership began to pass from father to son(s). Among the later scions of these noble families of East European Jewry were some remarkable spiritual figures, but also quite a few who were only pale reflectors of a greatness long past.

A *rebbe* does not necessarily possess formal rabbinic ordination. In any case, his role has little to do with deciding matters of law. (A Hasidic court might have its own *posek*, or legal decision maker, an ordained *rav** from within the Hasidic group.) The *rebbe's* follow-

ers believe that he serves as a channel of divine teaching and blessing. They gather around his *Shabbat** table to hear him "say
Torah*." They also come to him for blessings, especially when they
are in need. The *ḥasid,* on visiting the *rebbe,* will have a petition
written out bearing his or her name and mother's name along with
the matter in which the *rebbe's* help is being sought. In a private
interview, considered the heart of the master/disciple relationship,
the *ḥasid* will bare his soul to the *rebbe,* who in turn will offer
advice, support, and a promise of prayer on the *ḥasid's* behalf.

Especially in later times, some Hasidic rabbis have also been
men of great learning. Many are ordained rabbis who serve in a
combination of the *rav* and *rebbe* roles. As Hasidism, in the 19th
century, turned into a bastion of ultra-Orthodoxy and resistance to
change, respect for rabbinic learning grew higher within Hasidic
circles.

The modern rabbi is a spiritual descendant of both *rav* and
rebbe. The pastoral aspects of the modern rabbinate, including the
personal counseling and care shown to congregants, place today's
rabbi in the tradition, however transformed, of the Hasidic *rebbe.*
As contemporary Jews quest for ultimate meaning and personal
warmth and acceptance, it is often the skills of the *rebbe* that are
needed to do the rabbi's job.

שלום

Shalom

SHALOM or "peace" is Judaism's highest aspiration for the world in which we live. It is a value that is placed above all others. Rabbinic teaching describes it as the only "vessel" through which God's blessing can flow into this world.

Shalom as a value permeates every level of existence. Not only nations but groups of all sorts need to learn to live in shalom with one another. The usual opposite of shalom in classical Hebrew is not milḥamah ("war") but maḥloket, which means divisiveness or quarrel. Shalom means living in harmony with one another; maḥloket means division, sometimes leading to hostility, between people. Social, ethnic, and religious differences will exist until mashiaḥ* comes. Our job is to learn to live in shalom with others so that we help to bring about that redemption sooner.

The opposition of shalom and maḥloket exists on the personal level as well. Shalom bayit, or peace in the home, has an important place in the Jewish hierarchy of values. Many things may be sacrificed for its sake. This is primarily depicted as peace between husband and wife, but applies equally to parents, children, and others who share a home together. Volatile tempers are to be controlled rather than vented. Domestic violence, while it surely exists among Jews, is considered a deep violation of the Jewish sense of what home should be.

Shalom is a value within the individual person as well. In our complex world we are too torn between conflicting goals, values, dreams, and aspirations. Shalom is related to shelemut, meaning "wholeness." We need to set our course and live it wholly. Shalom with oneself and with God are impossible without one another.

שמחה

Simḥah

Simḥah or "joy" is the attitude toward life that Judaism seeks to instill. Despite the fact that Jewish history contains more than its fair share of bleak and depressing chapters, the tradition is a joyous one. The glory of singing "Holy, holy, holy" to God each day, along with the chorus of angels (*kadosh**), outweighs any price we have had to pay on the historical plane for the privilege of being Jews.

Prayer requires joy, say the rabbis. The best way to come to prayer is from the joy of having performed a *mitsvah**. This phrase *simḥah shel mitsvah*, "the joy of doing good deeds," is widely used in Jewish sources to describe the ideal state of human existence. Living in a way that fulfills the purpose of our existence should fill our hearts with joy.

Joy is a gift that we seem to receive in varied measures. There are some who are naturally joyous, who fill up with happiness at the simplest stimulation. Others struggle their whole lives to overcome a natural tendency toward depression; for them a moment of true joy is a rare event, one long anticipated and long remembered. This latter group has a special *rebbe** within Jewish tradition. Rabbi Naḥman of Bratslav (he lived in the Ukraine from 1772 to 1810) spent much of his life struggling for joy. His teachings on the subject are especially moving because they are deeply personal. Rabbi Naḥman taught that you must never let up in the quest for joy and that you have to chase after your own sadness in order to forcibly transform it too into joy. He offers the parable of a person who stands aside from a circle of dancers, too sad to join. Finally someone takes hold of the person, forcing him to join. As he dances, he notices his former sadness looking wistfully and somewhat disapprovingly at this new behavior. The task, says Rabbi Naḥman, is to bring that sadness itself into the circle and to see that it too is transformed into joy.

One type of *simḥah* belongs to the lone individual, the joy that fills us as we behold the beauties of God's world or bask in the blessings of one we love. Another *simḥah* needs to be shared with others in a more public way. This is the *simḥah* of a joyous occasion such as a birth, a marriage, a coming together of friends. Here the event itself is called a *simḥah*, "a joy." When we Jews see each other either at these events or, God forbid, on sad occasions, we greet each other by saying (in Yiddish) *nor oif simkhes*, which can be roughly translated as: "Here's hoping we see each other only at 'joys'!"

תלמיד חכם
Talmid Ḥakham

THE *TALMID ḤAKHAM* or "disciple of the wise" is the ideal of rabbinic society. The early rabbis defined their community as one of masters and disciples, *ḥakhamim* or sages and their pupils. The young scholar was encouraged to go forth— "Exile yourself to a place of *Torah**"—in order to find the proper teacher. The image of these teachers and their communities of disciples was drawn in the early *aggadah**, and certain distinctive characteristics came to be associated with them. These included extreme enthusiasm about learning and dedication to the point of self-sacrifice. The tales also record incredible feats of memorization and other sorts of knowledge.

The mature scholar, on the other hand, is described as a figure of great caution and sobriety. He does not rush into judgment. The *talmid ḥakham* knows how to include subjective factors when judging between humans and how to sidestep the setting of dangerous precedents. He is always aware that true justice belongs to God, for Whose law he is acting as a mere human agent. Nevertheless, he has the responsibility to act in determining the law, even when doing so requires great courage.

In the religious/intellectual tradition of Judaism, no distinction is possible between "scholar" and "sage." Learning, the acquisition and contemplation of Torah knowledge, makes us wise. Since primordial, universal wisdom and Torah are really the same, knowing Torah and knowing the world are one. For a few interesting and venturous souls over the centuries, this has meant that worldly learning of all sorts is for the good, since it leads to deeper understanding of God's Torah-created world. But for many more within the tradition, identifying Torah with wisdom meant that there was no reason to go beyond specifically Jewish learning, because "there is nothing that is not hinted at in the Torah."

The *talmid ḥakham* as Judaism's ideal type has been challenged over the centuries by both the *tsaddik** or righteous holy man, and the *ḥasid** who represents extreme piety or love of God. The history of Hasidism, perhaps the strongest witness to such a challenge, tells us that after a few generations' struggle a new synthesis or integration of the various types emerges on the scene. Something similar may be happening today in the Sephardic revival in Israel, where the veneration once given to popular *tsaddikim* is being transferred to classical *talmid ḥakham* types in a renewal of rabbinic leadership.

תיקון עולם
Tikkun 'Olam

TIKKUN 'OLAM, which means "mending the world," is an ancient Hebrew phrase that has taken on new life in the past few decades. Its verbal form is found in the 'alenu prayer, which concludes every service in the traditional synagogue. There le-takken 'olam means "to establish the world in the kingdom of the Almighty (shaddai*)," or to bring about God's rule on earth. In contemporary usage it refers to the betterment of the world, including the relief of human suffering, the achievement of peace and mutual respect among peoples, and the protection of the planet itself from destruction.

While associating these ideals with tikkun 'olam may be a recent innovation, the values themselves are deeply rooted in Jewish tradition. Spreading our most basic moral message—that every person is the divine image (tselem elohim*)—requires that Jews be concerned with the welfare, including the feeding, housing, and health of all. The Torah's* call that we "pursue justice, only justice" (Deuteronomy 16:20) demands that we work toward closing the terrible gaps, especially in learning and opportunity, that exist within our society and undermine our moral right to the relative wealth and comfort most of us enjoy. The very placing of humans on earth "to work and guard" (Genesis 2:15) God's garden, as well as the halakhah* forbidding wanton destruction of resources, tell us that protecting the natural order is also a part of that justice.

The rediscovery of ancient spiritual forms in recent decades has paralleled an age of activism for political and social change. In some cases these have been quite separate from, or even opposed to, one another. Many of those attracted to seeking spirituality have given up on the possibility of any serious improvement in the human condition altogether. In the case of Judaism, such a bifurcation of spiritual and sociopolitical concerns is hardly possible. Anyone who tries to undertake it ultimately has to deal with the prophets of ancient Israel, still the strongest and most uncompromising advocates for social justice our world has known. If you try to create a closed world of lovely Jewish piety and build it on foundations of injustice and the degradation of others, Isaiah and Amos will not let you sleep.

צַעַר בַּעֲלֵי חַיִּים

Tsa'ar Ba'aley Ḥayyim

"THE SUFFERING of living creatures"—*tsa'ar ba'aley ḥayyim*—is a moral domain to which pious Jews are supposed to pay attention. No animal creature (this includes fish and fowl) is to be caused unnecessary pain or tortured wantonly. While Judaism has accepted that domestic animals are to be raised and slaughtered for human consumption, the entire process is to be carried out in a manner that causes a minimum of suffering.

The *Torah** contains several laws that are generally interpreted to reflect these sensibilities. An ox may not be muzzled when being used to plow a field, and thus kept from eating the grass that lies plentifully before it (Deuteronomy 25:4). An animal and its offspring may not be slaughtered on the same day (Leviticus 22:28). A mother bird must be shooed away before you collect eggs from its nest; you may not take the mother bird along with the eggs (Deuteronomy 22:6–7).

Judaism rather grudgingly accepts animal consumption and its legitimization through ritual slaughter. Meat was permitted to humans, according to the rabbis, only after the flood, when God saw that the vegetarian ideal of Eden was not attainable by ordinary people. At this point the first universal law of kindness to animals was enacted, forbidding tearing a limb from a living creature. Then, according to Leviticus 17, the eating of meat was permitted only in a sacrificial context. Anyone who slaughtered an animal without bringing it to the priest was considered to have shed blood.

It is clear from several places in the legal texts of the Bible that the shedding of human blood and animal blood are related acts, joined together in a number of ways. Only in Deuteronomy 12 is the "profane" eating of domestic animals permitted, and then only because of the difficulties created by permitting a sacrificial altar only in Jerusalem, the ideal of the post-Davidic period.

Current Jewish law permits the use of animals for food, but remains concerned with the question of suffering. In recent years much concern has been raised over the way animals are placed into position for *kosher** slaughter, and some changes have been introduced. Using and killing animals for experimentation in areas where human life might be prolonged is also permitted. At the same time, the principle of *tsa'ar ba'aley ḥayyim* demands that such animals be treated kindly, and with awareness of their suffering, while alive. Great challenges to this principle of Jewish ethics lie ahead in areas such as transplants from animals and the possibility of "farming" animals who will exist solely to serve as sources of transplantable tissue or organs.

Tsaddik

TSADDIK or "Righteous One" occupies the place in Judaism held by the "holy man," spiritual master, or shaman in most of the world's religious traditions. But one is called a *tsaddik* primarily due to acts of extraordinary generosity and selflessness within the human community. This reflects the special character of Judaism as shaped by the prophets. Although many see such people as performing miracles and displaying special holiness, the Jewish figure is not generally called a *ba'al mofet* ("miracle worker") or a *kadosh* ("saint"), but rather a *tsaddik*. The Jewish holy man is thus defined by righteousness rather than by charismatic insight or special powers.

The Biblical paradigm for Judaism's rich *tsaddik* literature is the tales of Elijah and Elisha (I Kings 17–II Kings 9), which also served the creative needs of early Christianity. These were prophets who stood up to kings and queens, but who also cared for poor widows and hungry children. The *tsaddik* as he emerges in the *Talmud** and *Midrash** has great influence in the heavenly court. He can nullify divine decrees or even dictate to God orders to be fulfilled. But he would rather find himself in the marketplace, seeing to it that the poor are not cheated or that the needy are being helped in one way or another.

Essential to the character of the *tsaddik* is humility (*'anavah**), and that means an aversion to being publicly identified as a doer of good deeds. Early Jewish *tsaddik* tales are often about *nistarim*, "hidden ones," saintly figures who are known only by the fine aroma of goodness that they leave in their wake. At some point in the Middle Ages, Jews came to believe that there was a fixed number of thirty-six hidden *tsaddikim* in each generation, by whose merit the world continued to exist.

This usage of the term *tsaddik* as extraordinary holy man should not be confused with another meaning: *tsaddik* simply as "innocent," in the forensic sense, or "not guilty." That usage has the world divided between *tsaddikim* and *resha'im,* the "innocent" and the "guilty" or "wicked." But not every one free of sin is capable of the great feats that can be accomplished by the true hidden *tsaddikim.*

Tsaddik does not play a major role in any formal presentation of Judaism, either medieval or modern. No special note is taken of *tsaddikim* in *halakhah*,* which mostly passes over them in silence. But on the level of folk belief, Jews far and wide were inspired by tales of *tsaddikim,* sought them out during their lifetimes, and made pilgrimages to their graves. This is especially true of the Judaism practiced in the Ukraine, Morocco, and the Holy Land.

Hasidism marks a very important change in the history of the *tsaddik* and his place within Judaism. Rather than accepting the role of hidden righteous ones, the populist revival of Hasidism sought to make the *tsaddik* into a public figure. Only a true *tsaddik* is fit to serve as a leader and model for other Jews, it was argued. The Jews of Hasidic Eastern Europe came to be organized into tribes of disciples (*ḥasid**) following their respective masters. In many cases, such leadership tended to become dynastic. But even a Hasidic *rebbe** in later times would not be referred to as a *tsaddik* unless some unusual feats of goodness could be attributed to him.

Tsedakah

TSEDAKAH or "righteousness" is described by the prophets of Israel as belonging to the highest values of the religious life. It is often coupled with *mishpat* or "justice." Other terms associated with it are uprightness, perfection, straightforwardness. It is the path taken by the *tsaddikim** and those who seek to emulate their ways.

In the prophetic writings it is hard to distinguish between *tsedek,* the parallel masculine form of the noun, and *tsedakah*. Both seem to have the same range of meanings. But in later Hebrew usage, the feminine form *tsedakah* comes to be associated with a virtue of righteous generosity, a way of improving the world's balance specifically by giving to those who have too little.

Tsedakah may be performed either with one's own person, by doing for those who are in need, or with one's possessions, by giving to the needy of one's worldly goods. The fact that *tsedakah* often comes to be associated exclusively with the latter should not obscure its broader origins. Because *tsedakah* is more than just a financial commitment, the obligation to do it falls on everyone, including the poorest.

The recipients of *tsedakah,* those who depend upon the generosity of others, are a wide-ranging group. They certainly include the very poor, the homeless, and those unable to earn their livelihood. *Tsedakah* at one time included areas of "social needs" or "social services" that are today handled (with varying degrees of success) by various agencies of government. But the "needy" who receive *tsedakah* have also come to be defined as the educationally, emotionally, and spiritually hungry as well as those who literally cry out for bread. While *tsedakah* may never neglect the needs of those who are poor, it has come to include support of educational institutions, counseling facilities, and responses to many other human needs.

Being seen as a *ba'al tsedakah* (a "master of righteousness") or a "giver" in the Jewish community sometimes puts one into a difficult position. There are hundreds of causes, a great many of them worthwhile, and they all seem to pursue the same givers. To divide our ability to give by all the many causes that approach us can make each gift too small to be significant, while to give to one and ignore all the others seems somewhat heartless. It was for this reason, to avoid excessive competition among causes, that Jewish charitable federations were first established. The local federation will accept a gift and divide it between various local and worldwide needs. Many smaller funds exist that do the same thing, sometimes with a particularly interesting slant. This writer is personally partial to Danny Siegel's Ziv Tsedakah Fund (*Information:* Naomi Eisenberger, administrator; 384 Wyoming Avenue, Millburn, NJ 07041), which specializes in Israel and in causes of interest to children in the U.S. and elsewhere. Check them out!

עֶלֶם אֱלֹהִים

Tselem Elohim

THE BELIEF that every person is a *tselem elohim* or an "image of God" is the most fundamental moral claim of Judaism and its basis for a universal interpersonal ethic. In a now famous Talmudic (*Talmud**) debate, Rabbi Akiva proclaimed that "Love your neighbor as yourself" (Leviticus 19:18) is "the most basic rule of Scripture." His colleague Ben Azai answered that "This is the book of the generations of Adam" is a still more basic teaching. He was referring to Genesis 5:1–2: "This is the book of the generations of Adam; on the day when God created Adam He created him in the image of God. Male and female He created them and He blessed them, calling them 'Adam' on the day He made them." Ben Azai is warning Akiva, the great romantic, that love will not suffice as the basis of ethics. There are human beings one simply cannot love, or moments where love wears so thin that it cannot be relied upon. Even in moments such as these, he insists, one has to recall that the other is God's image and treat him or her as such.

The universality of God's image leads to the ethical norm of *kevod ha-beriot,* respect for all persons. Every human being has a right to such basic needs as food, shelter, work to sustain oneself without the gifts of others, and respect. Seeing that these are shared throughout humanity is the duty of all. The belief that each person is God's image will lead us to an abhorrence of all forms of human degradation, including slavery, prostitution, and addiction, where the sense of human dignity is so readily lost.

My teacher Rabbi Abraham Joshua Heschel ז"ל used to say that the reason we are forbidden to *make* graven images of God is that we ourselves *are* images of God. The point of the second of the Ten Commandments is not that God is imageless, but rather that to make a true image of God you need to use the medium of your entire life. Nothing less will do.

Great ethical questions remain in our day that cannot be solved simply by insisting upon the truth of *tselem elohim*. Does the belief that each life is God's image lead us to a total rejection of abortion? Not necessarily, because the child to be born must come into a life that will treat him or her as God's image. But is the person "God's image" even before birth? What does our faith in *tselem elohim* tell us about euthanasia? Does brain death mean the end of God's image in the person, or is a breathing being without hope of consciousness still the image of God? These questions are not answered by the essential ethical claim, but it provides the proper Jewish framework for their discussion.

עֲנִיעוּת

Tseni'ut

Tseni'ut or "modesty" is an important value of traditional Jewish society. It combines a shunning of public display of our own assets and accomplishments, a strong sense of privacy, and a constant awareness of what is appropriate to the public and private realms.

It is in the realm of dress that *tseni'ut* is best known to many Jews. Among the ultra-Orthodox, this tends to be defined as long sleeves, high necklines, and low hems for women, and long pants and jackets for men. These standards also imply that loose-fitting and nonrevealing garments are more proper.

Outside the ultra-Orthodox community, concerns for *tseni'ut* often center around the synagogue and what is appropriate dress for such religious occasions as synagogue services, weddings, or *bnai mitsvah (bar/bat mitsvah*)*. The rules here are less fixed, but there is a definite sense of propriety; any excessive display of the body, especially such as might be considered vulgar, should be avoided.

Less well known is the sense that ostentation as well as vulgarity is offensive to Jewish values. *Tseni'ut* applies not only to the body and to clothing, but to wealth and possessions as well. It means not only that the sexual allure of the human body should be preserved for bedroom privacy, but also that public displays of wealth and luxury are inappropriate behavior in a Jewish community. Wealth in itself is not frowned upon by Judaism, but it should be seen as an opportunity for giving and sharing (*tsedakah**) rather than as an occasion for display.

ישיבה

Yeshivah

A *YESHIVAH* is a school or academy for traditional Jewish learning. The term goes back to the academies of Babylonia in the early centuries of the Common Era. The Aramaic equivalent of the word, *metivta,* is also sometimes used. Literally *yeshivah* means "sitting" and is probably most directly parallel to the English word "session," which derives from "sit." The *yeshivah* was the assembly of scholars and students in session; only later did it refer to a specific place, institution, or building.

The curriculum of the *yeshivah* is largely devoted to the study of *Talmud*,* with emphasis on its legal sections (*halakhah**). Originally an oral enterprise involving impressive feats of memory, *yeshivah* study was transformed by the decision (probably in the 5th or 6th century) to commit the "oral *Torah**" to writing and again by the invention of printing in the 15th century. Nevertheless, memorization and oral fluency remain highly regarded in the *yeshivah*. They are valued along with intellectual acumen or "sharpness" as the chief skills of a successful *yeshivah* scholar.

Yeshivot have existed in Jewish communities far and wide for nearly two thousand years and there has been a good deal of cultural diversity among them. The *yeshivah* in various Sephardic communities often included *Kabbalah** alongside Talmud within its curriculum. *Yeshivot* in some times and places also included systematic study of Hebrew language and Bible. The *yeshivah* as it exists today is primarily modeled on a revival of the institution that took place in Lithuania and Poland in the 19th century. The Lithuanian *yeshivah,* beginning with that of Volozhyn, was inspired by the ideal of pure Talmudic learning for its own sake as cultivated in that community. While the training of future communal rabbis takes place there, the *yeshivah* is not at all seen as a professional school. In fact the rabbinate as a source of livelihood has been looked down upon by many of its finest graduates. Similarly, the determination of Jewish law for practical purposes is not considered the business of the *yeshivah*. The rabbi who serves as *rosh yeshivah* or dean of the academy may be called upon to reply to such questions and his responsa (answers to halakhic inquiries) might be eagerly read and discussed by his students. But even this is taken as a distraction from the true business of learning, conducted on a theoretical plane that assumes an open "contemporaneous" relationship among Talmudic masters, medieval commentators, and present-day students. Any reality that impinges on this living dialogue that takes place across the centuries remains foreign to the heart of *yeshivah* learning.

ישראל

Yisrael

THE JEWISH PEOPLE are called "Israel" after our ancestor Jacob, who was also called Israel. We are called by his name, rather than that of the other patriarchs or matriarchs, because his entire progeny formed the Jewish people. Abraham is the father of both Isaac and Ishmael, traditionally the progenitor of the Arabs and by extension the Muslim peoples. Isaac and Rebekkah are the parents of both Jacob and Esau, the ancestor of Rome and, as later understood, of Christendom. Rachel and Leah each mothered only a portion of the tribes of Israel. The tradition thus recognizes the common origins of all Western religions. We Jews are spiritual cousins—fellow descendants of Abraham—with those who follow Christianity and Islam. But the *immediate* family of Israel is that of Jacob's children. Therefore we are called by his name.

The *Torah** (Genesis 32:29) explains this name as coming from the root שׂ-ר-ר/s-r-r which means "to struggle" or "to be powerful." Jacob is given this name by the angel with whom he wrestles, "for you have struggled with God and with men and have prevailed." Israel would then mean something like "the people that struggles with God" or "wrestlers with the Mighty One." This is indeed a fitting name, since it is broad enough to include challengers, doubters, and heretics of all sorts, as long as they somehow remain engaged in the struggle with God. It is in faithfulness to this name that Jews insist on including doubters and even deniers as part of their religious community. Anyone still struggling with questions of religious truth may be part of a community with such a name.

An alternative reading that goes back as far as Philo (1st century B.C.E.) derives the name *Yisra'el* from another root, שׂ-ו-ר/sh-u-r, meaning "to see." According to this tradition, the people of

Israel are "the people who see God" or who stand directly in God's presence. All of Israel were to "appear before the Lord" three times each year, according to the Torah (Exodus 34:23; Deuteronomy 16:16). But a careful reading of those Torah passages shows that they originally meant "Israel *will see* the Lord." Being part of Israel means participating in the collective religious vision of the Jewish people. It means to see that God is with us. We are those who together "saw" God's presence at Mount Sinai, an event at which every Jewish soul (including future converts!) was—and is—present. It is an event that happens through all eternity.

A contemporary understanding of the name "Israel" would do well to combine the two traditions. The "struggle" and the "vision" need one another; each alone is incomplete. We struggle with our doubts and with our self-assurance, wrestling to the ground both our questions and our satisfaction with easy answers. We strive forever to achieve a closer, more intimate picture of the One and at the same time seek to maintain a pure and abstract understanding of what we mean by "God." Israel might thus be translated to mean "those who wrest a vision from the Lord."

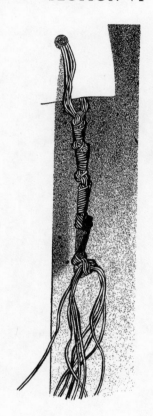

תשמישי מצוה וקדושה
Holy Things

אַרוֹן קֹדֶשׁ

Aron Kodesh

AN *ARON KODESH*, literally a "holy cabinet," is the ark in which *Torah** scrolls are kept in the synagogue. Though most commonly made of wood, it may be fashioned of any material that can hold the scrolls securely and respectfully. The front of the *aron kodesh* is usually covered with a curtain called a *parokhet*. This curtain is pulled aside when the *aron kodesh* is opened, either to remove one or more scrolls or at certain other dramatic highlights of the prayer service. The scrolls in the *aron kodesh* are the closest thing Judaism permits to a representation of God's presence in the synagogue. In moments of supplication, especially on the High Holy Days, the congregation stands directly before them.

The curtain-covered ark in the synagogue is based on the ark of acacia wood that was present in Moses' tabernacle (Exodus 25:10–22; 26:31–33) and Solomon's Temple (I Kings 8:1–11). The synagogue (*bet kenesset**) is a "lesser sanctuary." While not having the powerful holiness of the ordained Temple, its sacred furnishings are intended to recall the lost glory of those that existed in Temple times.

Because the *aron kodesh* holds the sacred scrolls, it too is to be treated as a holy object. Pious Jews kiss the *parokhet* as they come to the front of the synagogue. Dramatic moments of special prayer—such as those for rain in times of drought—once called for the removal of the *aron kodesh* (or *tevah*, a term still preferred in Sephardic speech) to the town square for public, outdoor prayers. Today the doors of the ark are opened for such special prayers. When all the Torah scrolls are removed from the ark, as on *Simḥat Torah**, a *ḥumash** is placed inside it so that it not be deprived of its task of housing the word of God.

חופה

Ḥuppah

THE ḤUPPAH or "canopy" is the central symbol of *nisu'in**, the Jewish marriage ceremony. "Coming to the *ḥuppah*" is a common way of referring to marriage. The *ḥuppah* actually represents the new home that the couple have prepared for themselves. To enter under the *ḥuppah* is to leave the parental home (during the betrothal year it was once traditional to live with the bride's family) and to symbolically come into the home and the new life-stage it represents. Thus developed the custom of parents leading bride and groom to the *ḥuppah* and staying behind as they enter beneath it.

The *ḥuppah* is a very ancient and universal symbol of Jewish marriage. Biblical verses (Psalm 19:6; Joel 2:16) attest to its existence even in the earliest times. One of them describes the rising sun as being "like a bridegroom, coming forth from his canopy." We have no evidence of what constituted a *ḥuppah* in ancient times, but it is likely that floral decorations were always part of it. In Roman times Jewish brides and grooms wore crowns or wreaths of flowers and it may be that the *ḥuppah* was similarly decorated.

In the mystical tradition, the *ḥuppah* is seen as *shekhinah**, the hovering presence of God, protecting the couple. To come under the *ḥuppah* is to be surrounded by divine light, a light that is also found in the *sukkah** and in the coming of *Shabbat* (*Kabbalat Shabbat**). The moment of marriage is one of life's great transitions and is not without its dangers. The Divine Presence promises that the union of these two souls will be for the good, furthering the presence of God's light and blessing in the world.

לולב/אתרוג

Lulav/Etrog

FOR THE FESTIVAL of *Sukkot**, the *Torah** tells us to rejoice by taking four species of growing things: the fruit of a lovely tree, assumed to be an *etrog* or citron, palm branches (*lulav*), myrtle twigs, and willows. The three latter species are joined together in a bundle and held, together with the *etrog*, for a special blessing (*berakhah**) and while reciting the *hallel**. They are also carried on a paradelike circling of the synagogue, while supplications called *hosha'not* are recited.

The origins of this *mitsvah** are obscure. The tradition of waving the *lulav* in all directions during the *hallel* is ancient and mysterious. It may be descended from a sort of rain-dance, invoking the winds or clouds to come from all sides to start the rainy season. The fact that the species mentioned grow in desert oases and are not those usually cultivated by farmers may point to *Sukkot*'s origin in recalling the desert wanderings of our ancestors.

The *Midrash** seeks various explanations of the so-called *arba'ah minim* or four species. Two of these explanations have enjoyed great popularity among Jewish preachers of all ages. According to the first, the *etrog* represents the heart, the *lulav* the spine, the myrtle leaf the eye, and the willow the mouth. All of these must be joined together in faithful service of God. According to the other explanation, four types of Jews are seen in the four species. The *etrog* has both aroma and taste, representing the Jews who have both good deeds and learning. The palm has taste but no aroma, like those who have learning but no good deeds. The myrtle, with smell but no taste, represents the goodly who are, alas, unlearned. Finally the humble willow, having neither taste nor smell, is like those Jews lacking in both areas. The point is that all four must be joined together so that Jews of varying kinds care for and give to one another. Many variants of these explanations have been elaborated over the centuries.

Kabbalah* contains extensive discussions of the four species. These begin with a *midrash* that sees all four of the species as representing God. For the kabbalist, the joining together of the species brings together the *sefirot**. The *lulav* represents *tif'eret*, the backbone of the sefirotic world. The myrtle and willow, which are attached to the *lulav*, are the *sefirot* of right and left. The *etrog* stands for *malkhut*, the feminine, embodied also in the Community of Israel. She is separable from the others, and therefore Israel (and the human soul) is in exile. By holding the *etrog* together with the bundle of palm, myrtle, and willows we symbolically bring about their union and thus the end of exile and alienation.

Matzah

MATZAH is traditionally called "poor people's bread" or "the bread of affliction." It represents the lowly food our enslaved ancestors had to eat in the Land of Egypt. It is completely simple, containing only flour and water, and is mixed, kneaded, prepared, and baked quickly (all in under eighteen minutes) so that it is given no chance to rise or ferment. Such rising is compared to the swelling of pride; *matzah* represents the person who maintains a humble (*'anavah**) and simple sense of self.

At the same time, *matzah* commemorates the dough our ancestors carried on their backs as they *left* Egypt. Having "made no provisions for the way" (because once you ask "What will we eat out there?" you'll never leave Egypt, says Rabbi Naḥman of Bratslav, the famous Hasidic master), they let the unrisen dough on their backs be baked by the sun's rays. Thus the same *matzah* represents affliction and slavery, on the one hand, and liberation and the return to the wilderness on the other.

On its most primitive level, *matzah* may have originally represented nomads' bread, which was baked by the sun before there were ovens. This fact was only later associated with the tale of the Exodus. Our wandering ancestors settled in the land and became farmers, but they still longed for the freedom of the "good old days" when they were nomads, following either the voice of God or the call of their own inner stirrings in moving about the wilderness. Once a year, at the time of the first spring full moon, they ate the old unrisen nomads' bread for a week; at the fall full moon (*Sukkot**) they expressed the same longing by living for a week in nomads' tents.

Jewish mystical teaching refers to *matzah* as "the food of [spiritual] health" and as "the food of faith." This symbolism has been seen as parallel to that of the Christian sacrament. *Matzah* is here seen as the precursor of manna, the gift of faith by which the people of Israel were sustained throughout their wanderings. Ingesting *matzah*, especially on the first two nights of *Pesah**, is itself seen as a holy act that confirms faith and makes us trust in God as our only true Provider.

Matzah shemurah is *matzah* made from wheat that has been especially guarded, ideally from the moment of harvesting, to be sure that no water has come in contact with it that might inadvertently have begun a process of fermentation.

Matzot mitzvah are the three *matzot* set aside for use during the *Pesah seder**. They are called by the names of the three groups of Jews: *Kohen* (or "priest"), Levite, and ordinary Israelite. Many families today that use regular machine-baked *matzah* for general eating will use hand-baked, round *matzah shemurah* for the *matzot mitzvah*.

Megillah

MEGILLAH means "scroll." It refers especially to *Megillat Esther,* the Biblical Book of Esther, which is read in the synagogue on *Purim** from a handwritten parchment scroll. The laws for writing and public reading from the *megillah* are quite strict, despite the levity associated with Purim.

The Book of Esther, according to the *Talmud**, was one of the last Biblical books to be included in the canon. The name of God never appears in the *megillah,* and some people undoubtedly read it as a purely secular tale of how the clever and daring exploits of Esther and Mordecai defeated the wicked Haman. Later Jewish tradition, however, does just the opposite. *Megillat Esther* is seen as documentation of the "hidden miracle," the unseen hand of God working through human agency and the historical process. For an age that does not experience obvious miracles, this witness is more important than any other. Interpreters rivaled one another at seeking out hints of Divine Presence from "behind" the seemingly profane *megillah* text.

Megillah (plural: *megillot*) can also refer to Esther and four other short Biblical books (Song of Songs, Ruth, Lamentations, and Ecclesiastes or Koheleth), which were also traditionally written as scrolls. Each of these books is read in the synagogue during the course of the liturgical year: Song of Songs on *Pesah**, Ruth on *Shavu'ot**, Lamentations on *Tish'ah be-Av**, and Koheleth on *Sukkot**. Collectively these books are known as the *hamesh megillot* ("five scrolls").

In Yiddish usage, *megillah* comes to mean an overly long and detailed story. This meaning is based on the model of the complicated Esther plot.

מְנוֹרָה

Menorah

A MENORAH is a lamp or candelabrum. The word is used in the Torah* regarding the seven-branched gold candelabrum (Exodus 25:31-40) of the tabernacle (mishkan*). It is also used today to refer to the eight-light Hanukkah* candelabrum.

The symbolism of light is very much present at the heart of Judaism. Dawn and dusk are times of prayer because of the mysterious changes in the light. Candles at the beginning and end of a holy time set off the sacred from the profane. The light of the first day of Creation, a light that preceded sun and moon, is hidden away for the future. It is a light we cannot see. "Light dwells with Him" says the visionary (Daniel 2:22). The aggadah* claims that the Temple windows were so constructed as to let the divine light shine out to the world, rather than to bring light into the Temple.

The menorah of the tabernacle and Temple in this sense almost seems superfluous. What need does a God Who shines forth with light and creates light have of our meager candles or our lamps? This question is raised in the Midrash* and answered with a parable of a great king who still loves his humble servants' gifts, even though he in fact has no need for them. The gift of light may be seen as a human attempt to give to God something that approaches divinity itself in fineness and abstraction.

The form of the menorah is derived from the shape of a burning or lighted tree. This is related to an ancient image of God as a cosmic tree or Torah as a tree of life. The divine tree bears light into the world. These images are much elaborated in later Kabbalah*, but seem to be of very ancient origin.

מזוזה

Mezuzah

A *MEZUZAH* is a strip of parchment, usually enclosed in a case, placed on the right doorpost of a house or room as one enters it. It is inscribed with the two passages from the *Torah**—Deuteronomy 6:4–9 (*shema'**) and 11:13–21—that mention the commandment "you shall write them upon the doorposts of your house."

The word *mezuzah* originally referred to the doorpost itself. During the Exodus from Egypt, the Israelite slaves were commanded to place the blood of the paschal sacrifice upon the lintel and doorposts of their homes so that they would be protected from destruction by the plague that killed the first-born of Egypt (Exodus 12:7). While the Torah offers no linkage between this story and the later commandment to write God's word upon the doorpost, the association is often made by later sources.

The *mezuzah* undoubtedly originated as an amulet of protection. Passage from indoors to outdoors, or the opposite, is a moment of transition that needs to be guarded. The fact that the divine name *shaddai**, which also stands as an abbreviation for "guardian of Israel's doorways," is written on the outer face of the *mezuzah* attests to this function. Typically, however, later Judaism re-interpreted the *mezuzah* as a token of Jewish home values. A home or room marked by a *mezuzah* is one where the teachings of Judaism are lived and practiced.

נרות שבת

Nerot Shabbat

NEROT SHABBAT or *Shabbat** candles are nowhere mentioned in Scripture. The *Torah** says only that one is not to light a fire on the Sabbath (Exodus 35:3). This meant that the evening lamp for Friday night had to be lighted before sunset, earlier than on other evenings. Because the Biblical law was also extended to mean that one could not feed the lamp or trim the wick on the Sabbath, a good strong fuel and proper wicking were needed to keep families from having to spend the night in darkness. This seems to be the origin of *nerot shabbat,* which eventually became a key household ritual and even a symbol of Judaism.

Shabbat is described as a time of light and joy. It was considered proper, even when the cost of lighting was dear, to try to have extra light in the house on Sabbath eve. Much later, perhaps only in recent centuries, it became traditional for Jewish households to have special candlesticks as ritual objects that would be used only for *Shabbat* and holiday candles. Shining silver or brass *Shabbat* candlesticks were the prized possession of many an otherwise impoverished Jewish home.

The designation of lighting *nerot shabbat* as a *mitsvah** to be fulfilled by women (and by men only if living alone or if the woman of the house is unable to do so) is of obscure origin. Women were generally the ones who took care of household lighting. There may also be an association with Proverbs 31:18, which describes the good wife as one whose "lamp does not go out at night." In any case, the lighting of *nerot shabbat* is listed as early as the *Mishnah** as one of the primary *mitsvot* to be performed by women. The tradition of candle lighting as the final act of preparation for the Sabbath was passed down from mothers to daughters. Among the *tehinot** there are many prayers that were written to be recited by women when lighting candles. This is also a time for private and spontaneous prayer. The lighting of candles is often preceded by giving *tsedakah**. After the candles are lighted and the blessing (following the lighting) is recited, the person who lights them has received the Sabbath and may no longer do any work, even if the sun has not yet set.

שׁוֹפָר

Shofar

A SHOFAR is a ram's horn. It is blown in the synagogue as the highlight of worship on *Rosh Hashanah** and is also used to announce the conclusion of *Yom Kippur**. Traditionally it is also blown each weekday morning during the month of *Elul* as a way of preparing for *Rosh Hashanah*.

The sounding of the *shofar* is considered an act of great mystery. The wordless but wailing *shofar* sounds are taken to be a "higher" or deeper expression of Israel's outcry than words can express. While the liturgy of *Rosh Hashanah* is perhaps the most eloquent and poetic of the year, the raw emotion of the season ("Thank You for bringing us alive to this time! Give us another year of life!") is so elemental and primitive that it is better expressed by these unrefined cries of the horn than by words of great poets.

The mystics attributed great significance to the order of the *shofar* blasts. One such *kavvanah**, attributed to Rabbi Isaiah Horowitz (who lived in Prague and Jerusalem in the 17th century), notes that each group of sounds begins with a *teki'ah*, a whole note, proceeds to *shevarim*, a "broken" note, divided into three parts, or even to *teru'ah*, an entirely fragmented sound, at least seven very brief sounds. But each broken note is followed by a whole note, another *teki'ah*. This, he says, is the message of *Rosh Hashanah*: "I started off whole, I became broken, even splintered into fragments, but I shall become whole again! I shall become whole again!"

Sukkah

A SUKKAH is a frail booth or hut, constructed outdoors in a spot unobstructed from above, where the fall holiday of *Sukkot** is celebrated. Ideally each family has its own *sukkah,* which becomes its temporary home for the week. All meals are served there (except during severe rain); guests are invited and all socializing takes place in the *sukkah.* Some families move beds to the *sukkah* and sleep there as well.

The *sukkah* is said to represent the booths in which the People of Israel lived during the forty years of wandering before entering the Holy Land. It also represents the farmer's hut, erected in remote corners of the field so that workers during the harvest might have shelter from the hot sun. While *Sukkot* is a joyous celebration of the harvest's bounty, the *sukkah* also has about it a certain frailty and otherworldliness. "Leave your ordinary home and dwell in this temporary home," the *Talmud** teaches. But the little *sukkah,* as it turns out, has all we need, causing us to question our dependence on all the comforts of our homes that we now leave so readily. Our trust in the *sukkah* as shelter is likened to our trust in God: Seemingly frail, it withstands great winds, especially if it is left open. The *sukkah* is also a symbol of peace, a humble home in which all are welcome and where divisions seem to be lessened.

The *sukkah,* erected before the holiday begins, is to be a temporary dwelling. It must have at least two full walls and a third partial wall, but may be left open on one and a half sides. Its roof is to be made from vegetable materials only, usually branches or mats laid across a few wooden poles. Though simple in construction, many *sukkot* are graced by beautiful decorations and wall hangings, giving a sense of elegance to the simple outdoor home.

טלית

Tallit

A *TALLIT* is a ritual garment, square or rectangular in shape. From each of its four corners, a tasseled fringe is suspended. These fulfill the commandment of Numbers 15:38, to wear fringes on the corners of our garments. Looking at the fringes or *tsitsit,* we are to remember the God Who brought us forth from Egypt and ordained for us a life of holiness. The *tallit* is worn by adults (in some communities only after marriage) during prayers. A lesser *tallit,* a rectangular fringed undershirt with a cutout for the head, is worn by pious men and boys throughout the day. The wearing of a *tallit* by women is a recent innovation, now widely accepted outside Orthodoxy.

While the ostensible purpose of the *tallit* is only to bear the fringes, which are the object of Biblical commandment (only a four-cornered garment requires fringes), the donning and wearing of the *tallit* itself has been given significance in the liturgy. Before wrapping ourselves in the *tallit,* prior to the morning service, we recite the opening verses of Psalm 104:

> Bless the Lord, O my soul.
> Lord my God, You are very great!
> You stretch forth the light like a garment;
> You unfurl the heavens like a curtain.

As the *tallit* is then unfurled and wrapped around the body, we are clearly copying the act of God in Creation. The *tallit* should ideally be put on just before dawn, when the first light of day appears. An ancient *midrash*,* commenting on these verses in the Psalm, reads: "Whence was the light created? God wrapped Himself up like the leader of the congregation and His garment shone from one end of the world to the other." One might then say that the imitation is mutual: God dresses like a prayer leader to create the light and we, greeting the dawn, dress ourselves as God did in Creation. After reciting the statutory blessing for the commandment of *tsitsit,* it is traditional to wrap one's head completely in the *tallit* and proceed with Psalm 36:8–11, beginning: "How precious is your love, O God, humans are sheltered in the shadow of Your wings." Here too it is clear that the *tallit* represents the garment of God, and wrapping ourselves in it is being wrapped in God's own loving presence.

תפילין

Tefillin

TEFILLIN are small square leather boxes that contain miniature parchments inscribed with certain Biblical verses. They are attached by leather straps to the forehead and upper arm. *Tefillin* are traditionally put on each morning, except on Sabbaths (*Shabbat**) and major festivals, and worn through the morning service. They are understood to fulfill the commandment "you shall bind them for a sign upon your hand and they shall be bands between your eyes" (Deuteronomy 6:8), although the rabbis acknowledge that no further evidence of the wearing of *tefillin* is found in the Bible.

The meaning of *tefillin* is symbolic and inspirational. Both mind and deed, head and hand, should be directed by the word of God and used to fulfill God's will. The wearing of *tefillin* symbolically transforms the human body into an instrument of active Divine Presence in this physical world. The validity of that symbolism is only tested, of course, by the moral life lived each day long after the *tefillin* have been removed.

Tefillin originated as amulets; the Greek term "phylacteries," now used in English as well, attests to that meaning. The Jews of late antiquity began a process that transformed a protective device into a statement of witness: The person who wears *tefillin* seeks to fulfill the divine words that are contained within them.

The *tefillin* contain the four Biblical passages that refer to *tefillin*: Exodus 13:1–10, 11–16 and Deuteronomy 6:4–9 and 11:13–21. In the *tefillah* on the head, each verse is contained in a separate compartment, while in the hand *tefillah* they are all together on a single parchment. As thought is turned into deed, some interpreters say, its disparate strands are united.

The *Talmud** claims that God too wears *tefillin*. These contain the verse "Who is like Your people Israel, a unique nation upon the earth" (I Chronicles 17:21). Thus *tefillin* serve as a mutual testament to the love of God and Israel. This passage in the Talmud is highly valued in the mystical tradition, where *tefillin* are seen as akin to radio receivers, external devices that can help the wearer receive the ever flowing blessing of God as it comes into the world. While knowing full well that it is in truth the open heart that is the recipient of these blessings, great emphasis is placed on *tefillin* as outward receptors of that inward grace.

SECTION VII

מקומות קדש
Holy Places

בריאה

Beri'ah

BERI'AH means "Creation." It refers both to the *act* of God creating the world and to the *object* of Creation, the universe itself. All that exists is the creation of God, sustained in each moment by the constant love of God for all creatures, or the flow of divine energy into the world. We say in the daily *shaḥarit** service that God "renews each day, constantly, the act of Creation." Unlike the creation of a human artist, God's fashioning the world out of nothing is an eternal process, not just a one-time event. God is *always* creating the world. We acknowledge God as Creator through our love and respect for God's Creation.

There is no word for "nature" in classical Hebrew, since the very idea of nature is derived from Greek rather than Hebrew thinking. (The term *teva',* which is used in modern Hebrew for "nature," is a creation of medieval translators who needed a word to use when translating Greek and Arabic philosophical writings into Hebrew.) "Nature" would imply a world separate from God, governed by its own internal rules. Neither the Bible nor the early rabbis had such a concept. The world and all that it contains is divine Creation.

Creation is a long-neglected issue in Jewish theology. Most Jews do not literally believe that the world was created in seven days, about 5,760 years ago. We generally turn to science rather than to the *tanakh** to understand *how* the world came into being. But *why* it and we exist remains the ultimate religious question. Because the *how* and the *why* cannot be completely separated from one another, the relationship of God to the origins of being requires careful and profound thought. What room is there for God within or alongside the evolutionary process? Can there be a purpose or ultimate meaning to an existence that came about and continues to develop as described by science? Or do we need to live with a bifurcated mind, accepting scientific method for understanding the world's origins, but then turning to a different mode of consciousness when we seek to appreciate or express our love for that same universe?

These questions do not have easy answers. Resolving them has to do not only with Judaism's future, but with humanity's ability to find a religious language that will inspire us to preserve our world and pass on a habitable planet as a legacy to future generations. Key to this language, from a Jewish point of view, is our awareness that "the whole earth is full of God's glory" and that all of Creation is a testament to God's ceaseless handiwork.

בית המקדש
Bet ha-Mikdash

BET HA-MIKDASH is the ancient Temple of Jerusalem, the central shrine of the Israelite nation. Two Temples were built on the same site—Mount Moriah—which is allegedly where Abraham had shown his willingness to offer Isaac as a sacrifice. The First Temple was built by King Solomon and is described in II Kings 6–8. That Temple was destroyed by the armies of Nebuchadnezzar of Babylon in 587 B.C.E. About fifty years later, after the Persian conquest of Babylon, the generation of the "return to Zion" began to build the Second Temple, a significantly smaller and less glorious building than its predecessor. The construction and dedication of the Second Temple are described in the Book of Nehemiah. That Temple was desecrated by the Seleucid rulers and rededicated by the Hasmoneans in 165 B.C.E. (*Hanukkah**). It was expanded by Herod in the last pre-Christian century but was then destroyed by the Romans in the great siege of Jerusalem in 70 C.E. Traditional Jewish belief claims that a third Temple on that site will be erected by God in messianic (*mashiaḥ**) times or, according to some more fanciful sources, will descend fully built from heaven and alight on Mount Moriah. There is no call in classical Judaism for the building of a third Temple in pre-messianic times.

The primary form of worship in *bet ha-mikdash* was sacrificial. Daily offerings at dawn and dusk, augmented by additional sacrifices for Sabbaths (*Shabbat**), new moons (*Rosh Ḥodesh**), and festivals were the collective gift of the people Israel for the maintenance of their world and their covenant with *Y–H–W–H**. These animal sacrifices took the place of the forbidden shedding of human life-blood, which had been eliminated by the very story of Abraham and Isaac that had first sanctified this altar. The

sacrificial killing of animals, many of which were used for food
(*kosher, kashrut**), was accompanied by meal offerings from the
poor, libations of wine and water, and the singing of the chorus of
Levites or Temple singers. We do not know of prayers recited by
the priests in the First or early Second Temple. Some claim that
the rites were mostly conducted in silence. The innermost sanctum of the Temple was the holy of holies, entered only once a year
by the high priest for the purification rites of *Yom Kippur**.

In addition to these formal communal rites, the Temple was also
the site of daily offerings by individuals, either as atonement for sin
or as personal gifts of thanksgiving. The faith that God was pleased
by sacrificial gifts, and especially that divine anger at human sin
could be alleviated by offerings, was common to almost the
entirety of the ancient world, including Israel.

In the last two to three centuries of the Second Temple's
existence there began to grow, alongside the religion of *bet ha-
mikdash*, a new sort of faith and religious expression. This was a
religion based on the study of Scripture and the recital of verbal
prayers. It was led by laymen, who were increasingly more
respected for learning and piety than for priestly or royal lineage.
In its most extreme forms, in fact, it was anti-priestly, or at least
believed the Jerusalem priesthood to be entirely corrupt. The more
moderate form of this new religious tendency was led by brother-
hoods (*ḥavurah**) of Pharisees ("separatists"), who were the spiritual ancestors of the early rabbis. During the final decades before
the destruction of the Second Temple, there was a synagogue or
place of rabbinic study and prayer even on the Temple Mount
itself.

After the Temple was destroyed, the rabbis mourned it deeply,
offering no sense that it represented a form of religion whose time
had passed. In this they embodied the religious and national feelings of the Jewish people as they faced exile. They claimed that
their prayer rites, which had actually developed quite indepen-
dently of the Temple, could serve to replace the sacrifices. But they
insisted that this replacement was only a temporary one. The

critique of the corrupt Temple cult was now mostly silenced as nostalgia for lost grandeur became the reigning emotion. This remained the case throughout the long Jewish diaspora. Although many Jews certainly shared the view of Maimonides that sacrifice had been a divine concession to the needs of our ancestors and that prayer represented a more advanced stage in human worship, the traditional prayer book (*siddur**) continues to include prayers for the re-institution of sacrifice in the Temple of the messianic future. Most non-Orthodox prayer books have eliminated those passages.

בית כנסת

Bet Kenesset

A *BET KENESSET* is a synagogue. Literally the term means "assembly house" and probably referred to the single public building of a given Jewish community, used daily for prayer but also for other gatherings of the entire Jewish community. The *bet kenesset* may be small or large, a grand building made for prayer and communal assembly or the gathering place of only a *minyan** of Jews. (Yiddish distinguishes between a *shul,* a building erected or totally dedicated to public prayer and related purposes, and a *shtibl,* a room or a residence partly converted for use as a place for a smaller group's prayer.)

A *bet kenesset* is considered a holy place, but only in a semi-formal way. No one is excluded from the synagogue because of ritual impurity (*taharah/tum'ah**) and non-Jews are permitted to visit and attend all services. The tradition of washing hands upon entering the *bet kenesset* continues today only in parts of the Orthodox community. The *bet kenesset* is referred to by the ancient sources as *mikdash me'at,* "the lesser sanctuary," meaning that its holiness derives from that of the ancient Temple, but is not comparable to it.

There are, nevertheless, rules of conduct that apply to the regular place of prayer. These include modest dress (*tseni'ut**), restrictions on profane speech and on conversation altogether during prayer and *Torah** reading, and generally respectful deportment. Jewish communities vary greatly in the degree to which these restrictions are followed. Some of these rules may also be extended to a temporary *bet kenesset,* a place where a *minyan* of Jews and a Torah scroll are present and used for worship.

אֶרֶץ יִשְׂרָאֵל

Erets Yisra'el

ERETS YISRA'EL, the Land of Israel, has been a central focus of Jewish dreams and aspirations since Biblical times. It is the land where Abraham wandered, dug wells, and tended his flocks. It is the land God promised to Abraham's descendants, who would return to it after a long period of exile and enslavement. It was the vision of life in this glorious land that inspired the slaves to go forth with Moses from Egypt and sustained them through their years in the wilderness. Joshua's conquest of the land, followed by long struggles with Philistines and other tribes indigenous to *Erets Yisra'el*, led to the first Jewish commonwealth, the kingdom of David and Solomon in the 10th century B.C.E.

A thorough intermingling of history and legend, this tale has inspired Jews living some 3,000 years later to return to our never-forgotten land and re-assert Jewish rule over it. But the relationship between the Jewish claim to the land, the question of divine promise, the special conditions of living in this land, and the very notion of what we mean by "holy land" all need clarification.

The *tanakh** refers to the land in early times as the Land of Canaan. After the conquest by Joshua it is called *Erets Yisra'el*. Sometimes the Divine Voice calls it "My land." Only very rarely does the Bible use the phrase "holy land." Nevertheless the land is treated as a divine gift to Israel. God keeps some special watch over this land and what takes place in it (Deuteronomy 11:12). Continued possession of *Erets Yisra'el* or exile from it depends upon the people's behavior. If they violate the covenant, the land will "spew them forth" (Leviticus 18:25, 28), as it did its former inhabitants.

The special status of the Land of Israel is conferred by God, not by us. Its holiness is not like that of *kiddushin*, the sanctification of marriage, where exclusive "possession" is implied. It is closer to that of a sacred object, which remains holy whether Jews possess it or not. A *Torah** scroll, preserved in a non-Jewish library for centuries, retains its holiness even though it may continue to be owned by others. The land remained holy even through our long exile, when our connection to it was only one of dreams and imagination. Its holiness today does not depend upon Jewish ownership or rule. The State of Israel is a great historic achievement of the Jewish people. Its role in the survival and renewal of Jewish life, especially in the aftermath of the Holocaust, cannot be overestimated. But the state as such has no *theological* significance. *Erets Yisra'el* is holy with or without Jewish rule. The laws of *shemitah** and other special agricultural restrictions will apply to Jews living in Palestinian-ruled parts of the land no differently from those who live within Israel's borders.

Holiness (*kadosh, kedushah**) belongs only to God. When something of that holiness is lent to an earthly entity, such as a holy people, a holy day, or a holy land, it is to teach some great lesson about all of life, not just about that holy entity. The way we treat *Shabbat**, for example, should teach us how to love and sanctify all of time. Every day potentially has the same value and beauty that *Shabbat* has, but we learn about it through setting one day aside for special treatment. In the same way, all land should be treated with reverence and care. We are taught this through the special example of *Erets Yisra'el*. The message is meant to go through the specific to the universal.

What is the message of the Jewish people's return to the Holy Land in this century? We live in a period torn by constant ethnic strife. Every group wants its own territory, its own power, and tends to set its own needs far above those of others around it. But in our day, thanks to the dangers of "advanced" weaponry, any of these ethnic conflicts could threaten our shared earthly habitat altogether. The earth lives in a state of extreme precariousness, due to our inability to resolve the age-old pattern of one human family set against another. In the midst of all this, the Jewish people returns to *Erets Yisra'el,* entering into what may be the seemingly most intractable of all such conflicts. The message in this situation is almost too obvious to need saying. How do we live in a holy land in our time? How do we show the world what it is to live in a place that is holy? The answer is that we do so by *sharing* it with others.

The seeming simplicity of this message is not to say that our politics need to be naive or simplistic. We have been placed among genuinely difficult neighbors, and we have not been such easy neighbors ourselves. Many among our neighbors would like to see us destroyed or removed altogether from this land. The military strength and vigilance that have been developed by the State of Israel over its first half-century of existence have been vital to its survival. But we who continue to think of *Erets Yisra'el* in terms of covenant or sacred trust believe that the *purpose* of that survival has to be more than just survival itself. We remain a kingdom of priests (Exodus 19:6) devoted to a message about a single God (*shema'**) and the creation of all humans in God's image (*tselem elohim**). Real enemies test our faith in that message every day. The ultimate victory of Israel (people, state, and land) lies in our ability to keep faith with our message and act upon it here in the real, tough world of interpersonal and political life.

כותל מערבי
Kotel Ma'aravi

THE *KOTEL MA'ARAVI* or "Western Wall" was one of the outer supporting walls of the Temple Mount in King Herod's rebuilt Second Temple (*bet ha-mikdash**), dating from 20–15 B.C.E. Traditionally it was thought to be the only wall left standing of the Second Temple, and the rabbis said that "the *shekhinah** never departed from the Western Wall."

Beginning in the early Middle Ages, the Western Wall served as a focal point for Jewish pilgrimages to Jerusalem. By Muslim ordinance as well as by *halakhah**, Jews were not permitted to enter the Temple Mount area itself. But the Western Wall, which was just outside the former Temple grounds, was considered a holy place, one especially to mourn the Temple's destruction and to pray for its restoration. These tearful supplications gave rise to its designation as "Wailing Wall" in English and other western languages.

The *Kotel* continued to be a place of traditional prayer under Arab, Turkish, and British rule in Jerusalem. It was mainly a place to recite *tehillim** or for small *minyanim* (*minyan**) to meet informally for prayer. Public prayers on a large scale were mostly unknown there, partly because the *Kotel* faced a narrow alley and there was no space for large assemblages. Following the Jordanian conquest of the Old City of Jerusalem in 1948, Jews (including those with foreign passports) were not permitted access to the Kotel for nineteen years. This turned it into a fervently regarded national as well as religious symbol. When the Old City was conquered in the 1967 Six Day War, the *Kotel* was seen to have been "liberated" from foreign control. The Israeli army's chief rabbi blew the *shofar** there, calling the moment the beginning of redemption. Within a short time, several blocks of houses in front of the *Kotel* were removed, creating a large plaza where mass gatherings could take place.

In a process lasting many centuries, it seemed that Jewish civilization was one that had made a transition from a spatially-based to a temporally-based orientation. While we still revered the place of our ancient Temple, *Shabbat** as holy day had become much more vital to the lives of Jews than Jerusalem or the *Kotel Ma'aravi* as geographical center. But the strong revival of Judaism that has taken place since 1967 has lent a great deal of importance to sacred space. The notion of "pilgrimage" to Israel, whether for *bar/bat mitsvah**, with a youth group, or in an adult Jewish Federation "mission," has become quite widespread. Inevitably, a visit to the *Kotel Ma'aravi* is seen as a (and perhaps *the*) highlight of such a pilgrimage. The Jewish people has decided by its actions that it once again has a sacred center in the geographical sense, and that is the *Kotel* and the plaza before it.

Because the *Kotel* has become such an important universal symbol for Jews, the exclusive domination of religious life there by the ultra-Orthodox rabbinate has become a sore spot for some. Various incidents in which female and non-Orthodox prayer groups have been attacked have received wide publicity.

מקוה

Mikveh

THE TERM *MIKVEH* means "gathering of waters." It occurs in the third day of the Creation story (Genesis 1:10), where it is said that "God called the gathering of waters 'seas.'" An ancient play on words connects this meaning of *mikveh* to another, which is "hope." Thus, "the Lord is Israel's hope" (Jeremiah 13:17) is taken also to mean "the Lord is Israel's *mikveh*" or place of purification.

In rabbinic Hebrew *mikveh* refers to a ritual bath, a pool that contains at least forty *se'ah* (about eighty gallons) of naturally gathered waters. These may be flowing from a river, lake, or stream, as long as the body of water is undammed. In the more usual case of an artificially constructed bathhouse, rainwater has to drain into the bath without artificial pumping. Other water may be added to the forty *se'ah* in order to render the bath large enough for comfortable use.

Immersion in the *mikveh* is a form of ritual purification. The *mikveh* is used by women preparing for sexual contact with their husbands, either directly before marriage or seven days after the conclusion of their monthly menstrual flow. Biblical law seems to require men to immerse in the same way after each seminal emission, but the practice was not enforced as *halakhah** developed in post-Talmudic (*Talmud**) times. Hasidic men and others of exceptional piety still use the *mikveh* for this purpose, immersing themselves each morning before prayer. Male immersion in the *mikveh* is more widely practiced on the eves of major holidays as a way of preparing to enter a higher state of holiness.

The requirement that women cleanse themselves in the *mikveh* has to do with the very pervasive taboo against contact with blood in the Biblical ritual mindset. The requirement of this *mitsvah** only of women has been much criticized in some feminist circles, where it is taken to show the control male authorities have sought to assert over women's bodies. Others, while not denying this historical dimension, have tried to reshape the ritual of monthly immersion into a celebration of feminine uniqueness and closeness to the divine as it is present in such natural phenomena as the flow of water.

משכן

Mishkan

MISHKAN means "dwelling-place" and refers specifically to the tabernacle or tent of meeting that accompanied Israel through their forty-year wanderings in the wilderness. The portable structure contained a number of separate areas, bearing successive degrees of holiness as one entered further inward. At the center of the *mishkan* lay the Holy of Holies, to be entered only once a year on *Yom Kippur** by the high priest. This area lay directly before the ark (*aron kodesh**), where the stone tablets of Sinai, Israel's most precious possession, were kept.

The word is derived from the root שׁ-כ-ן/sh-k-n which means "to dwell." *Shakhen* from this root means "neighbor." *Shekhinah** is the Divine Presence that fills the *mishkan,* described as "glory" in the *Torah**. The Divine Presence, dwelling in our midst, is as close as one who stands right next to you.

Exodus 25:8, the commandment to erect the *mishkan,* reads: "Let them make me a holy place and I will dwell in their midst." The Hebrew *be-tokham* ("in their midst") is ambiguous; it could also be translated "within them." From this has evolved a long tradition that reads this verse and the entire *mishkan* description to refer to an inward sanctuary, the true dwelling-place we make for God within the human heart. That *mishkan* too has outer and inner chambers, places we enter rarely and only with great preparation, and its innermost sanctum contains our most precious truths.

מִצְרַיִם

Mitsrayim

MITSRAYIM is "Egypt," the land where Israel escaped from bondage in the event that formed the people and its mission for all time. As a result, *Mitsrayim* itself exists as a negative symbol in the religious language of Jewry. This does not mean that Jews today bear any animus toward contemporary Egyptians. It was recognized long ago that Egypt itself had been transformed after the fall of the Pharaohs, and Jews lived peacefully among latter-day Egyptians for many centuries.

Mitsrayim is derived from the word meaning "strait," referring to the narrow strips of fertile land along the Nile, hemmed in by the desert. When we speak today about "coming out of Egypt" or the liberation we are to seek on *Pesaḥ**, those "straits" are usually reapplied to our own spiritual situation. What is it that is closing us in? In what places in our lives are we too tight, too constricted, unable to see or experience life broadly and open-handedly? Our *Mitsrayim* is an "Egypt" of the mind or soul from which we need to make the long trek to freedom.

Mitsrayim also means the place of oppression. Jews far from Egypt lived in *Mitsrayim* for many centuries, whether it was called Spain, Germany, Morocco, or Russia. As the tale of Exodus has become the property of all humanity, we see that such "Egyptian" bondage exists everywhere, including our own country. We just-liberated slaves are supposed to know what to do when we see it. Even when we are on the other side of the master-slave relationship, we cannot be blind to the familiar reality.

עולם הבא
'Olam ha-Ba

'OLAM HA-BA or "the world to come" is the usual Jewish term for life after death. It is widely believed in but little defined in traditional Jewish sources. It seems to be identical with *gan 'eden* or the Garden of Eden as the dwelling-place of the soul after death. The general popular belief seems to be that souls exist in this disembodied state until messiah (*mashiah**) comes. Grievous sinners suffer great pain in separation from the body, and the dead who lack in merit earned in this world may go through a year-long period of purgation in *Gehinom*. The soul is then purified and joined to those of the righteous in *'olam ha-ba*. At some point after messiah comes, the bodies of all will be resurrected (*tehiyat ha-metim*) and joined to their souls. Whether this renewed existence is eternal or only temporary, as suggested by Maimonides, is not spelled out in the sources. The many other obvious issues raised both by the question of nonbodily individuality and bodily resurrection are left unresolved as well.

Speculation about life after death has not been a great preoccupation among Jews. It is considered wrong to serve God for the sake of reward, and excessive concern with the nature of that reward is improper. Various folk beliefs have grown up around the afterlife, some of which may even contradict one another. Since there is no practical implication to such beliefs, *halakhah** has no interest in them and they remain quite entirely uncodified. Within a general framework of believing that the soul, which comes from God, is eternal, Judaism accepts a wide range of beliefs in this area. This includes various forms of belief in reincarnation and possession by spirits that are especially a part of the Kabbalistic (*Kabbalah**) tradition. Even the term *'olam ha-ba* is used in a variety of ways, sometimes referring to the afterlife of the individual soul but elsewhere to the messianic era on earth.

The Hebrew Bible (*tanakh**) in fact shows very little interest in the afterlife. The rewards for doing good and fulfilling the covenant are to be found in this world, in God's blessing upon us, our offspring, our people, and our land. The spirit is indeed from God, but "the body returns to dust whence it came and the spirit returns to God who gave it" (Ecclesiastes 12:7). According to one rabbinic source, there exists a divine entity called *guf* ("body") that contains within it all the souls that will exist until the end of time. Perhaps the souls of the dead return to that *guf*, constantly replenishing the supply and offering to future newborns some subtle taste or pre-conscious memory of what it is to live in this world. The collective life-experience of all who have lived, infinitely rich in variety and yet drained of all need for separateness, may live on as *tseror ha-ḥayyim*, the "bundle of life," into which all souls are drawn. That highly abstract notion of afterlife, one free of the ego-need for continued individuality, surely also has a home in Judaism.

יְרוּשָׁלַיִם

Yerushalayim

YERUSHALAYIM or Jerusalem is the city chosen by God to be His holy place. Other specific places may be holy because of ancient events, settlements, or associations. But only Jerusalem is "the city of God, His holy mountain; beautiful sight, joy of all the earth" (Psalm 48:2–3). Jerusalem is the center of Judaism's universal vision, spoken by the prophets of ancient Israel. The transformation of the world is to come forth from there:

> It shall be at the end of days
> That the mountain of the Lord's house
> Shall be established above all mountains,
> Exalted over all the hills.
> All nations shall flow there as rivers
> And many peoples shall go and say:
> "Come let us go to the mountain of the Lord
> To the house of the God of Jacob.
> He will teach us His ways
> And we shall walk in His paths."
> For teaching shall go forth from Zion
> And the word of the Lord from Jerusalem.
> He shall judge between the nations
> And decide among many peoples.
> They shall beat their swords into plowshares
> And their spears into pruning hooks.
> Nation shall not lift up sword against nation,
> Neither shall they learn war any more. (Isaiah 2:2–4)

Jerusalem thus lies at the very heart of Judaism's most universal vision, the vision of peace. This love for a particular holy place, a love we proclaim to be shared by God with countless generations of Jews, is an essential part of our spiritual identity. There is no understanding of Jews or Judaism without it. While we know full well that God is everywhere, accessible "to all who call upon God in truth" (Psalm 145:18), whoever and wherever they are, this city maintains a unique and central place in our religious imagination. Its welfare and especially its peace are of special concern, a regular object of Jewish prayer, both ancient and contemporary. The cry "Next year in Jerusalem!" with which we conclude both *Yom Kippur** and the *Pesaḥ* *seder**, is our fondest hope, our cry for redemption. Since the days of the prophets the redemption of Israel and the rebuilding of Jerusalem have been thoroughly identified with one another: "Break forth and rejoice together, O ruins of Jerusalem, for God has consoled His people, redeemed Jerusalem" (Isaiah 52:9).

All of the above was true and could have been written a hundred or even a thousand years ago. But over the past hundred years the Jewish people has changed its relationship with Jerusalem. In deciding not to wait for divine redemption, but to initiate the return to Zion on our own, we re-created an earthly and mostly Jewish city of Jerusalem. Those of us who are committed to Judaism have visited Jerusalem, perhaps lived there for a period, probably at least thought about living there forever. Jerusalem is a reality, a city with a mayor, traffic problems, a Jewish and an Arab population, crowded markets, religious/secular tensions reaching the level of hatred, and overbuilding that threatens its incredible natural beauty. It is also a city of endless Jewish spiritual, artistic, and intellectual riches. What does this real Jerusalem have to do with the Jerusalem of prophetic vision, prayer, and fantasy? How are the sublime vision and the concrete reality to be integrated?

Judaism insists that they are one. Our love is not for a heavenly Jerusalem but, in the words of Rabbi Naḥman of Bratslav, "these very stones, these very houses." In this we are unabashedly particularistic. Helping the poor of Jerusalem, building a synagogue in Jerusalem, bringing peace to Jerusalem, all mean more to us than those same activities anywhere else. In the same way, hearing that rights of non-Jews are being violated in Jerusalem or that injustice is being done there offends us more than it would anywhere else. Our very Jewish position as conquerors of an unwilling Arab minority in the Holy City makes the dream of Jerusalem as the city of peace seem farther from reality than ever.

In the face of a complex and bitterly contested reality (and these words are, of course, being written in Jerusalem) it seems important to take a stand. Let it be said clearly that the true Jewish vision of Jerusalem is not about exclusive domination. *Jerusalem belongs to God, not to us.* What we are supposed to create in Jerusalem is a teaching of peace, one that will lead all humans to love one another more, to make more room for difference. That is why we are here! We cannot do that by dominating, but only by sharing, by the example of making room for more than one in God's holy city.

We have before us a great challenge and a magnificent opportunity. We can show the world—including all those involved in seemingly irresolvable ethnic conflicts—that there is a way of living together, side-by-side, with one who has been a bitter enemy, and that there is a way to change the chemistry of our interactions through generosity and openness. Doing this would show that we are indeed free, no longer driven by the ghosts of our past and the fears that have so long haunted us. We have the power at this moment to make Isaiah's vision a reality, to show that out of our very particular love for Jerusalem can come a transformative lesson for all humanity. Or we can insist that it all belongs to us and just hunker down, fortify, build more Jewish neighborhoods on more dominant hilltops, and wait for the next war to come. Jerusalem remains the locus of our finest dreams, but only if we can overcome our worst nightmares.

מועדי קדש
Holy Times

בר מצוה/בת מצוה

Bar Mitsvah
Bat Mitsvah

BAR MITSVAH, one of the few terms for which no reader will require translation, has undergone a great shift in meaning in recent times. Properly the phrase refers neither to the ceremony nor to the event, but to the young lad himself. From the age of thirteen he is *bar*, which in the legal sense means "one liable to," *mitsvah**, which is used here collectively to refer to the commandments. In other words he becomes legally an adult and is responsible for his own religious and moral conduct. It became customary in recent centuries to celebrate this by calling upon the new *bar mitsvah* to read from the *Torah**. The child's father notes this change in status by thanking God "for releasing me from punishment for this one." *Bat mitsvah* has the same meaning with regard to the young woman: She is now liable to fulfill the commandments.

In Eastern Europe the new *bar mitsvah* was called upon to give a speech, usually a bit of Talmudic (*Talmud**) dialectics that was supposed to display his scholarly skills. Often this was in fact a set piece, memorized and barely comprehended by the young man. His family would then provide a modest *kiddush* or celebration at the synagogue in his honor.

The much caricatured, lavish *bar mitsvah* celebration is mostly a North American innovation. It began in the 1920s, a collaboration of nouveau-riche Jews wanting to flout their money, supported by caterers and others with commercial interest, ever willing to help in that effort. Synagogues were competing for members, and rabbis and educators were willing to put up with vulgarity and bad taste if they allowed for the Jewish education of generations of children. The synagogues' growing insistence that *bar mitsvah* required a certain number of years of Jewish education did much to keep the Hebrew schools in business.

A strange alliance was thus made between what might be called the best and worst elements of Jewish life. The genuine desire of families to see tradition continued and the great efforts of educators to teach language, religion, history, and Jewish identity to anxious and overburdened pre-adolescents were buttressed by the promise of a great party and a chance to display wealth and status. Today a new generation of Jewish parents, often more serious about their own Jewish lives, are working to sort out these elements and choose among them in creating a ceremony and a celebration that reflect their own values. Often this has come to include involving the young person in some active *tsedakah** project as a model of responsible Jewish adulthood.

Bat mitsvah, the parallel ceremony for girls, was created in the 1920s by Mordecai Kaplan, the innovative rabbi, educator, and theologian, who later founded the Reconstructionist Movement, and father of four daughters. Formal Jewish education for girls was a relatively new idea in the early 20th century and *bat mitsvah* remained extremely rare for decades after Kaplan started it. In the Reform Movement, where the *bar mitsvah* ceremony had been eliminated in favor of Confirmation at age fifteen or sixteen, girls often took an equal or leading role. The growth of the *bat mitsvah*, primarily from the 1950s onward, indicated an increasing commitment to gender equality in Jewish education. In earlier years, Conservative as well as modern Orthodox rabbis sought to make the *bat mitsvah* something other than a direct copy of the male ceremony, one with which many rabbis had become quite unhappy. These efforts generally failed, partly because of pressure from the growing feminist movement not to let *bat mitsvah* be anything "less" than the males' ceremony. Today in most non-Orthodox synagogues (Reform began re-instituting *bar mitsvah* and adding *bat*

mitsvah in the postwar decades) the *bar* and *bat mitsvah* ceremonies are usually identical. *Bat mitsvah* in modern Orthodox
circles often includes an *aliyah* for the girl's father, a talk or class
taught by the girl outside the context of the synagogue service, and
a celebration.

בְּרִית מִילָה

Brit Milah

Brit milah is the covenant of circumcision, also known as the covenant of Abraham our Father. Before Abraham's son Isaac was born, according to the *Torah**, Abraham was told to circumcise him and all future males of the tribe at the age of eight days. This was to be a sign of the covenant between God and Abraham, according to which Abraham and his descendants would fulfill God's will and the Lord would protect them and, after a period of exile, restore them to their land.

The marking of the covenant sign in the flesh of a newborn shows that Jewish generations are born into the covenant without choice. Membership in the covenantal community of Israel comes as birthright. It needs to be confirmed by study and commitment, but the absence of these does not suffice to nullify the very strong sense of family bond that creates the Jewish people, the earthly embodiment of this spiritual heritage. Originally this link was passed on from father to child. Later, in early rabbinic times, it came to be defined as a matrilineal linkage, passing from mother to sons and daughters both. Today there are many who say that Judaism may be passed through either parent, though that view is still highly controversial. But it is the Jewish father or, if there is none, the other closest Jewish male relative, who is obliged to see that the child is ritually circumcised.

Circumcision is usually performed by a *mohel* or professional circumciser, who serves as the father's agent. The brief ceremony is impressive and awesome. An elder, usually a grandfather or honored guest, is *sandek,* holding the baby for the rite. For a moment the child is placed on a specially designated chair called the "throne of Elijah," where Elijah the Prophet is said to hold the child on his lap, a sign of blessing and of the love of children that transcends all generations. Among the verses read is Ezekiel 16:6: "I passed by and saw you steeped in your blood and I said to you: 'By your blood you shall live; by your blood you shall live.'" As the last phrase is repeated, two drops of sweet red wine are placed on the infant's tongue, symbolically replenishing the drops of blood spilt in the circumcision. Circumcision is almost universal among Jewish males, despite conflicting medical opinions as to its value. Today there are many Jewish physicians who will perform circumcision for medical and ritual reasons both.

A parallel naming and blessing ceremony for newborn girls is a recent innovation, a result of the influence of feminism on Jewish life. Traditionally, baby girls were named by their fathers in the synagogue, though there is an old Sephardic custom of celebrating the event called *zeved ha-bat*. Various forms of the new naming rite for girls have been published over the past quarter century. Some involve immersion, washing of feet, or other use of water. All these recall female association with the *mikveh**. Others are more simple verbal and musical rites, and are often specially attuned to the family's religious tastes and needs.

חנוכה

Hanukkah

HANUKKAH (literally: "dedication") is an eight-day early winter festival that celebrates the victory of the Macabbean rebels over the Hellenistic Seleucid rulers in the year 165 B.C.E. The events of this period are recorded in the Books of the Maccabees, written in Greek and preserved in the Apochrypha (a collection of addenda to the Hebrew Bible). The Macabbean revolt was a nativist Jewish reaction to the increasing Hellenization of Judea and the threatened disappearance of the distinctive religious culture of the Jews. Under the leadership of the Hasmonean priestly family from Modi'in, the rebels won a surprising victory, initiating a period of relative independence for Judea that was to decline only with Roman domination about a century later.

Legend has it that when re-dedicating the Temple from pagan defilement, the Maccabees and their helpers found only a small flask of olive oil with the intact seal of the high priest, enough to last a single day. Miraculously the oil lasted eight days until a new supply could be obtained. Thus supposedly arose the practice of lighting candles on *Hanukkah*, with one additional candle added on each of the eight nights.

Historians of Judaism have come to believe that *Hanukkah* is based on an older winter festival, perhaps one that had pagan associations, later historicized by linkage with the Macabbean victory. The lighting of candles on winter nights, especially as the solstice is passed and days begin to grow longer, is a practice that has parallels in other parts of the world.

Hanukkah is considered one of the "minor" festivals of the Jewish calendar. Not being mentioned in the *Torah**, it involves no Torah-based commandments and no prohibition of work. In status it is often compared to *Purim**, another holiday celebrating a historic event—saving of the Jews from destruction—in post-Torah times. There are, however, several differences between the two. Purim's Book of Esther is in the Biblical canon and provides specific rules for celebration of the day. *Hanukkah's* origins are noncanonical; only in the *Talmud** does one find discussion of the *Hanukkah* lights and, incidental to these, the events themselves. Because *Purim* celebrates triumph over a threatened physical annihilation of the Jews, it is celebrated by feasting and drinking, but not with the recitation of *hallel**. *Hanukkah,* on which the primary threat was spiritual, is celebrated with *hallel* but not with special emphasis on food or drink.

In the past half century *Hanukkah* has gained in perceived importance by both Jews and non-Jews. The struggle for religious liberty that *Hanukkah* seems to portray is a very "American" theme, which Jews in the United States are quite comfortable and proud to share with others. The fact that *Hanukkah* occurs in December, when Jews in Christian countries are beset by the attractiveness of the Christmas season, has also raised its prominence considerably. The minor tradition of giving *Hanukkah gelt,* bits of small change with which children played gambling games, has been expanded into a major *Hanukkah* gift-giving tradition. In Israel *Hanukkah* has taken on great importance, and is read in Zionist terms as the struggle of Jews of an earlier generation in *Erets Yisrael** for both cultural and physical survival.

Levayah

LEVAYAH, the Hebrew word for "funeral," literally means "accompaniment." We accompany the deceased to his or her final resting place.

No Jew should die or be buried alone. We are born into a community with a strong sense of the passage of generations and the transmission of each generation's heritage. When the time of passing from this world comes, a community of Jews—at least a *minyan** of ten—should be there to accompany each person. This is a statement that the Jewish people feels and cares for each person within it. The presence of such a supportive community is also intended to help console the mourners themselves.

The essential *mitsvah** of attending a funeral is thus that of accompanying the deceased to the gravesite. The participants in such a procession, in addition to giving honor to the individual deceased, also acknowledge their own mortality, realizing that they too will one day take that final journey, accompanied by a similar procession.

Until the moment of interment, the body of the deceased is the central focus of a funeral service; *kevod ha-met* or respect for the dead is its governing principle. As soon as the grave is covered, however, concern shifts from the deceased to the surviving family. After burial there is no more we can do for the dead. From that moment, as we form two lines to surround the family leaving the cemetery, we begin the work of consolation.

Ne'ilah

THE CONCLUDING SERVICE of *Yom Kippur** is called *ne'ilah,* the "closing" or "locking" of gates. It is recited during the final hour of *Yom Kippur,* between dusk and nightfall. Its atmosphere combines passion, urgency, and exhaustion in the final effort of atonement. The various special lines within the *'amidah*,* recited from *Rosh Hashanah** through *Yom Kippur,* that call upon God to "inscribe" us in the book of life, are now changed to a plea that God "seal" us for life, since the heavenly books are sealed as *Yom Kippur* ends.

There is some debate among the commentators as to just what "closing of the gates" is meant by the name of this service. It would seem to refer to the heavenly gates through which prayer is received, and which are about to close with the end of the day. The problem with this reading is that heaven's gates don't really close. If the angels did try to close them at the end of *Yom Kippur,* we humans could always turn to tears (which some do anyway during *ne'ilah*) and the *Talmud** explicitly says that "the gates of tears are never closed." Other commentators therefore said that these were the gates of the earthly Temple; *ne'ilah* is recited at the hour when the Temple gates were usually closed.

That is an interesting fact, but hardly very impressive. Why should this prayer of the synagogue be timed to the closing of the Temple gates? It makes more sense to say that the prayer refers to the gates of our hearts, which are about to close up because we have reached the end of our ability to keep them open. The entire season of *Rosh Hashanah* and *Yom Kippur* has made great emotional demands on us. We stand face-to-face with our mortality, we examine the value of our lives, we pray for others who are dear to us. In this final hour, as we realize the inner gates will have to close, we begin to turn from supplication toward making peace. We start on the road to accepting the new year, whatever our fate in it will be. This acceptance, however, is one of joy, not of resignation. *Ne'ilah* concludes with a confident and ringing declaration of faith and a hopeful "Next year in Jerusalem!"

The real job of *Yom Kippur* is to show us that we are still capable of *teshuvah**, of growth and change. That is why the Book of Jonah is read in the *minḥah** service, immediately preceding *ne'ilah*. Jonah is a cynic; he does not believe that people will really change. The people of Nineveh are sinners and deserve to be punished. The prophet must learn that God, at least, continues to believe in these human creatures, including the possibility that they will change their lives and return to God. For that purpose, we need to be shown that our heart's gate remains open, that it is still capable of stretching and opening as wide as it ever has. This is the lesson of *ne'ilah*.

נישואין

Nisu'in

Nisu'in is the Hebrew term for the marriage ceremony, the greatest personal celebration known to Jews. The term actually means "uplifting," as bride and groom are "uplifted" from among all others by being chosen as marriage partners.

The marriage service as currently celebrated actually combines two ceremonies, originally held as long as a year apart from each other. The first, called *kiddushin,* was a formal betrothal rite. There the agreement to marry was made between the families and the woman was declared to be betrothed, often going to live in the home of her in-laws for the betrothal period. The marriage was concluded and celebrated at a second ceremony, *nisu'in.* Only after this were the couple permitted to be alone together. In later times, the two events were conflated into a single marriage service.

Weddings are the paradigm for all joyous events among Jews. Our most joyous songs are wedding songs; the most exuberant Jewish dancing is to be seen at weddings. This has to do with a belief that love is at the heart Judaism and the relationship of God and Israel is somehow like that of husband and wife (*Shir ha-Shirim**). But it also has to do with a great sense of the importance of continuity among Jews, as a small and often decimated people. The hope that a new generation will continue to carry forth Israel's sacred mission and bear the legacy of the past into the future is the great hope of Judaism. It is present at every Jewish marriage.

פסח

Pesaḥ

*P*ESAḤ is the festival of spring, liberation, and renewal. Since Biblical times, *Pesaḥ* has commemorated Israel's Exodus from Egypt, which is the paradigm for movements of national liberation as well as the great example for spiritual and personal liberation wherever the Bible is read and taught.

Pesaḥ is celebrated for seven days (plus one additional day in the diaspora, because of ancient calendrical uncertainties). The first night is marked by a festive *seder**, at which the legacy of slavery and the memory of liberation are passed down from one generation to the next. The *seder* is generally repeated on the second night in the diaspora. Reform Jews celebrate only a single *seder*. Throughout the week, following the Biblical injunction, no leaven or leavened products may be consumed, owned, or seen in a Jewish home. For traditional Jews this means a thorough housecleaning and changeover of everything related to food and food preparation. In its strictest form, this includes changing utensils, dishes, and all kitchenwares from those used during the year to special ones reserved for *Pesaḥ*. Even many who are lax about observing *kashrut* (*kosher**) during the year become quite strict in avoiding *ḥamets* (leaven) on *Pesaḥ*.

The liberation celebrated on *Pesaḥ* is primarily historical and national. But spiritual teachers, especially in the Hasidic tradition, have long understood it to refer to the liberation of each person from his or her own inner *Mitsrayim** (Egypt) as well. The mind is in exile, cut off from its own natural closeness to God, just as the body and the people suffer exile on the physical plane.

Underlying the "season of our freedom," as *Pesaḥ* is called by the rabbis, there may be a still older holiday, a spring full-moon festival featuring the slaughter of spring lambs, perhaps as a token replacement for the now taboo slaughter of the tribe's first-born sons. The slaying of Egypt's first-born, the blood on the doorposts of Israel on the Exodus night, and the *Torah's** insistence that only the circumcised may eat of the paschal lamb, all point to the presence of this distant pre-Israelite memory underlying the *Pesaḥ* story. One of Judaism's greatest gifts has been its ability to transform ancient memories of these half-forgotten rites, combined with the experience of historical suffering in Egypt, into a tale of freedom that continues to inspire the quest for liberation throughout the world.

פורים

Purim

THE FESTIVAL of *Purim* is celebrated on the 14th of *Adar,* usually corresponding to mid-March. In Jerusalem and other ancient walled cities, places similar to Shushan of the *Purim* story, it is celebrated a day later (Esther 9:18–22). *Purim* commemorates the events of the Biblical Book of Esther (*megillah**), the defeat of wicked Haman and the foiling of his plot to kill the Jews throughout the Persian Empire.

There are four *mitsvot* (*mitsvah**) associated with the celebration of *Purim.* All of them are already mentioned in the ninth chapter of the Book of Esther itself. These are the reading of the *megillah,* the exchanging of gifts (usually cakes and sweets), giving to the poor, and merry feasting. The last-mentioned often includes drinking, even to the point of *'adloyada,* "no longer knowing" the difference between "Blessed be Mordecai" and "Cursed be Haman." *Purim* feasting takes place at a special festive meal, *se'udat purim,* held in the home on the afternoon of *Purim* day, after the other *mitsvot* have already been discharged.

While there is no historical evidence to corroborate the events celebrated on *Purim,* the festival is a great favorite among Jews throughout the world. It is seen as testament to the overthrow of all the many foes and persecutors of the Jewish people. "So many Hamans," a Yiddish saying goes, "but only one *Purim.*" This same feeling caused the term "*purim*" to be used as a generic term for a day of salvation from enemies, and various communities in Europe celebrated local "*purims*" in memory of such events.

In addition to the essential *mitsvot* of the day, secular customs of various kinds have grown up around *Purim* and are widely observed. These include the *Purimshpiel,* a parodylike play at which authorities, enemies, etc. may be freely mocked. The *Purimshpiel* was among the earliest forms of Jewish theater. Both children and adults are permitted to dress in costume on *Purim*. In Tel Aviv, a carnival (called *'adloyada*) has been instituted, and the custom is now widely copied in local Jewish communities throughout the world.

Hasidic teaching sees *Purim* as a time of hidden miracles. The story of Esther, which appears as a mostly secular tale in the Bible, is used to show that the Divine Hand is present even in events that seem ordinary. Much is also made of the parallel between *Purim* and the holiest day of the Jewish year, *Yom Kippur**, sometimes referred to in the *Torah** as *yom kippurim,* intentionally misread to mean "a day like *Purim.*" Why is *Yom Kippur** like *Purim?* On *Purim,* we become so inebriated that we cannot tell Mordecai from Haman; on Yom Kippur, God becomes so "intoxicated" by the prayers of Israel that no distinction remains between the righteous and the wicked, and all are forgiven as one. On *Purim,* Jews used all their cleverness, along with divine help, to defeat our external enemies; on *Yom Kippur,* we call upon those same forces to defeat the evil urge, the "Haman" within the human heart.

ראש השנה

Rosh Hashanah

ROSH HASHANAH, literally the "head of the year," is also the Day of Judgment, the Day of Remembrance. Though not formally named as such, it is also the day of rebirth, the time of renewal. It is the first highlight of the fall festival season. The thirty penitential days of the month of *Elul* have led up to it, especially the last week of *Elul* (in the Ashkenazic tradition) when *seliḥot* or penitential hymns are chanted each day before dawn.

Rosh Hashanah, a two-day festival in Israel as well as in the diaspora (though celebrated for only one day by Reform Jews), begins the "ten days of return (*teshuvah**),*" which are also designated as *yamim nora'im,* "the Days of Awe." This is a season of high drama in the Jewish calendar. In a series of images adapted from the ancient Babylonians, God is said to be seated on the Throne of Judgment at this season. The heavens are conceived as a "courtroom" where each person's good and evil deeds are weighed in the balance. Angels act as prosecutors and defenders as the person's reward or punishment, primarily in the form of extended life or threatened death, is meted out. Repentance during the period between *Rosh Hashanah* and *Yom Kippur** (extended two more weeks by popular tradition, up to *Hosha'na Rabbah*) may improve one's chances, but at the conclusion of that time the decree is "sealed."

This long-popular depiction of *Rosh Hashanah* is not without its theological difficulties. What does it mean that a person's fate is "sealed" for the year? Is God not free to accept *teshuvah* at any time? And is the loving God not merciful to sinners even on these Days of Awe? Is the whole picture not too anthropomorphic and too paternalistic to allow for a mature religiosity? Might this not be a tale for children, inappropriately imposed upon the adult wor-shipper as well? Even for children, one might add, today's educa-tors would question whether the threat of judgment is a proper motivator for moral growth.

For these and other reasons, various interpreters tend to inter-nalize this imagery. The God of judgment stands for conscience; *Rosh Hashanah* becomes a time for self-examination and commit-ment to growth and change of habits. The essential statement of faith is that we *are* capable of change. God calls upon us, symboli-cally through this season but actually at all times, to be the best human beings, morally and spiritually, that we can be. This demands of us a constant openness to change and growth.

The special *mitsvah** of *Rosh Hashanah* is the sounding of the *shofar.** The prayer service of the day contains some of the most majestic Hebrew prose ever written. It includes a unique *mussaf** service of nine blessings. The middle three of these are especially devoted to themes of the season, each composed of a mosaic of ten Biblical verses. Each section is followed by the sounding of the *shofar.* The first is *malkhuyot* or "royal verses." The kingship of God, established since Creation, is the chief liturgical theme of *Rosh Hashanah,* the day that commemorates Creation. The second section is *zikhronot* or "memory verses." The same God who created the world remembers and cares for the destiny of all crea-tures. God remembers each of us just like Noah in the ark, Israel in Egypt, and all those who trust in God. The final group of verses are called *shofarot,* "shofar-sounding verses." The ram's horn that was sounded at Sinai will be heard once again as a sign of the com-ing redemption, toward which our prayers are turned.

The solemnity of the *Rosh Hashanah* prayers should not obscure the fact that this is a joyous festival as well. Jews greet one another with wishes for a good and "sweet" year. The theme of sweetness is carried over into culinary traditions. Both ḥallah (bread) and apples, dipped in honey, begin the *Rosh Hashanah* meal. In addi-tion, various foods prepared with honey are eaten.

ראש חודש

Rosh Ḥodesh

ROSH ḤODESH is the beginning of the Hebrew month. It is celebrated for either one or two days, depending on calendrical calculations. The Hebrew calendar being a lunar one, *Rosh Ḥodesh* is the day (or days) when the new moon first appears. The middle of the month (the date when several festivals occur) is the day of the full moon.

In Biblical times, *Rosh Ḥodesh* was celebrated as a holiday, a time of sacred assembly and special sacrificial rites. These are still reflected in the liturgy for *Rosh Ḥodesh,* but any real sense of celebration of the day has been lost. The New Moon did, however, come to be known as a time for women to express their piety, perhaps because of longstanding feminine symbolic association with the moon and the lunar cycle. It thus became traditional for unusually pious women to avoid work on this day, much as they would on a festival. In recent years feminist circles have adopted *Rosh Ḥodesh* as a time for special meetings and women's celebration.

The Kabbalists (*Kabbalah**) view the new moon as a time of relief from danger. The monthly diminishing of the moon until it is finally out of sight recalls an ancient legend about God punishing the moon because she wanted to rule equally with the sun. The moon is taken to be *shekhinah** and her disappearance reflects her subjugation to the forces of evil, a condition that God is said to regret and mourn. The moon's reappearance at *Rosh Ḥodesh* is thus a time for rejoicing and hope for that day when "she will no longer be diminished." Redemption will mean that *shekhinah* will no longer vanish from view and that God's presence will be felt and seen throughout the universe.

ספירת העומר
Sefirat ha-'Omer

THE "COUNTING of the *'omer*" derives from the Biblical commandment (Leviticus 23:15) to count fifty days from the morrow of the Sabbath (*Shabbat**) following the first barley offering to the festival of the first fruits (*Shavu'ot**), in Greek referred to as Pentecost (fiftieth) for this reason. The Pharisees and later the rabbis took that "Sabbath" to be the first day of Passover, even if it occurred on a weekday.

In traditional Jewish practice, the counting off of each day is performed as a ritual act, preceded by a blessing (*berakhah**). The counting is preferably done in the evening, after the stars have come out.

The weeks of the *'omer* counting are considered a minor time of mourning by traditional Jews. Weddings are not held, music is not played, and various other sorts of entertainment are avoided. Hair is not cut and some men do not trim their beards during the *sefirah* period, as it is called. The origins of this designation as a mourning period are obscure. One traditional explanation is that a plague killed many among the students of Rabbi Akiva, ceasing only on the thirty-third day (*Lag be-'Omer*), which is why the prohibitions of the season are canceled on (and some say: beginning on) that day. Anthropologists have pointed to a parallel spring mourning season (Christian Lent, for example) in many other cultures.

The Kabbalists (*Kabbalah**) associate each of the forty-nine days of *sefirat ha-'omer* with some combination of two of the seven lower *sefirot**. Thus the first day is *ḥesed* within *ḥesed*, a time of great grace, the second is *din* within *ḥesed*, a time of danger overcome, etc. Only following the final combination of *malkhut* within *malkhut*, the kingship of God fully affirmed, can *Shavu'ot* arrive and the giving of *Torah** be celebrated. Hasidic teaching sees the seven weeks as a period of purification during which Israel prepares to once again receive the Torah.

Shabbat

SHABBAT or the Sabbath is the central religious institution of rabbinic Judaism. Observance of *Shabbat* is the practice that most defines membership in the traditional community of the Jewish faithful. The idea of a holy day, unlike any notion of sacred place, is seen by the *Torah** as existing from the beginning of the world. It started on the day after humans were created, on the day God rested. God sanctified the Sabbath from the very beginning of time (Genesis 2:1-4). This is a way of saying that human existence itself cannot be imagined in a world where there is no *Shabbat*.

The root of the word *Shabbat* means to "cease" or "desist." To observe *Shabbat* means to cease our work life and break our daily routine every seventh day, making that day holy. *Shabbat* is to be a day of enjoying God's world rather than doing battle with it; a day of relaxation rather than struggle, a time to live in harmony rather than to achieve domination.

Two events are celebrated each *Shabbat*. One is God's Creation of the world. Our rest is a way of taking part in God's rest, even re-entering for a while the perfect garden God created this world to be. *Shabbat* is known as bearing within it "the taste of Eden" and "something of the World to Come (*'olam ha-ba**)," which is a renewed Garden of Eden. But *Shabbat* also commemorates the Exodus from Egypt (*Mitsrayim**). Slaves are not able to choose their rest. The ability to create one's own balance of work and leisure is a sign of freedom. According to the *Midrash**, Moses went to Pharaoh and demanded a weekly day of rest for the Hebrew slaves, thus instituting *Shabbat* even before they left Egypt. Part of each *Shabbat*'s celebration is based on our admitting that we are still slaves to work, oppressed today by the fast pace of our work lives and the pressures of living in a highly achievement-oriented society. Our taskmasters today may be electronic rather than human, tempting us rather than whipping us to work just a little faster and harder. Our ability to leave them behind once a week is our proclamation of freedom, a true cause for celebration.

The Torah gives almost no instructions about how to observe the Sabbath. "Work" is forbidden, but the nature of that work is not defined. A few details, including the forbidding of lighting fire and gathering wood on the Sabbath, are all the text provides. The rabbis, however, found an entire body of *Shabbat* law hidden in the Torah, based on a parallel between the *mel'akhah* ("work") prohibited on *Shabbat* and the work required for the building of the desert tabernacle (*mishkan**). All the forms of work required for the building (there are thirty-nine major categories and many derivatives from them) are those forbidden on the Sabbath.

The tabernacle, of course, stands for the Jerusalem Temple (*bet ha-mikdash**). In ancient times the religion of Israel was Temple-centered and the most vital rites took place only at that sacred place. All the rest of the world, as it were, was situated around it. (Since Christians inherited this sacred geography from the Jews, it is no surprise that the earliest maps show Jerusalem as the center of the world.) The rabbis of the 1st and 2nd centuries, facing the loss of the Temple, somehow understood that it needed to be replaced. A portable sacred center, one that sanctified time rather than space, could serve equally well in exile as in the Land, and would not threaten their ongoing commitment to Jerusalem (*Yerushalayim**). Ingeniously they tied the Sabbath to the Temple by employing the same set of rules. By *doing* this set of labors, we build sacred space; by *refraining* from the same list of labors, we hallow sacred time. *Shabbat* thus becomes a mirror image of the Temple, a tabernacle-in-exile that serves over the centuries as the actual center of Jewish life.

Shabbat may still be the most important religious form that Judaism has to give to humanity. In our age of ever increasing pace and demand, the need for a day of true rest is all the greater. But the forms of *Shabbat* observance as they have evolved in endless detail are, for many Jews, overwhelming and even oppressive to the very spirit of *Shabbat* freedom. A contemporary *Shabbat* will have to be a simplified and streamlined one. This is necessary before *Shabbat* can be accepted by larger parts of the Jewish people, and also for the sake of any new message of *Shabbat* we might hope to extend beyond the borders of Jewry. Such a *Shabbat* will, of course, have to be entirely voluntary, without compulsion of any sort.

In the spirit of fulfilling this need, I offer the following list of ten prescriptions for a contemporary *Shabbat*. They may be used either alone, to create a *Shabbat* for you and your family, or in combination with whatever traditional *halakhah** seems to work for you.

Ten Pathways toward a New Shabbat

DO:

1. STAY at home. Spend quality time with family and real friends.
2. CELEBRATE with others: at the table, in the synagogue, with your community or *ḥavurah**, or with those with whom you can best share in appreciating God's world.
3. STUDY or read something that will edify, challenge, or make you grow.
4. BE alone. Take some time for yourself. Check in with yourself. Review your week. Ask yourself where you are in your life.
5. MARK the beginning and end of this sacred time: lighting candles and *kiddush** on Friday night and *havdalah** on Saturday night.

DON'T:

6. Do anything you have to do for your work life. This includes obligatory reading, homework for kids (even without writing!), unwanted social obligations, and preparing for work as well as doing your job itself.
7. SPEND money. Separate completely from the commercial culture that so much surrounds us.
8. Do business. No calls to the broker, no following up on ads, no paying of bills. It can all wait.
9. TRAVEL. Avoid especially commercial places like airports, hotel check-ins, and similar depersonalizing commercial encounters. Stay free of situations in which people are likely to tell you to "have a nice day!" (*"Shabbat* already *is* a nice day, thank you!")
10. USE commercial or canned video entertainment, including TV and computer. Stay in situations where you can be face-to-face with those around you, rather than facing the all-powerful screen.

שבועות
Shavu'ot

SHAVU'OT, which is celebrated fifty-one days after the beginning of *Pesah**, is described in the Bible as an agricultural festival. The *Torah**'s fullest description of *Shavu'ot* (Deuteronomy 16:9–12) sees it as a joyous time celebrating the full growth of the crops. It is also the festival when the first fruits were brought to the Temple.

Only in post-Biblical writings does *Shavu'ot* come to be known as the day the Torah was given. In rabbinic Judaism, this is the chief meaning of the festival. Synagogues are decorated with green leaves. This recalls the outdoor setting of Mount Sinai. The Torah reading is from Exodus 19–20, the account of the giving of the Torah, followed by a *haftarah** from the first chapter of Ezekiel, the vision of the divine chariot, a repetition of the Sinai experience in the life of the individual prophet.

The Kabbalists (*Kabbalah**) originated a custom, now very widespread, of staying awake all night on *Shavu'ot* eve and studying Torah as preparation for receiving Torah once again at dawn. Although there are varied customs as to what is to be studied on that occasion, a special compilation called *Tikkun Leyl Shavu'ot* was created for this occasion, containing readings from each section of the Bible (*Tanakh**) as well as a sampling of rabbinic teachings.

The covenant at Sinai is often depicted as the symbolic marriage of God and the Jewish people. In Sephardic synagogues, a special *ketubah* or marriage contract is read in the synagogue to celebrate that occasion. It is also customary to read the Book of Ruth on *Shavu'ot* because the events of that story took place "at the beginning of the barley harvest" (Ruth 1:22). It is appropriate that Ruth, the symbolic mother of all converts to Judaism, be welcomed on the festival when the covenant of Sinai is renewed.

שמיני עצרת

Shemini 'Atseret

SHEMINI 'ATSERET is the eighth day from the start of *Sukkot**, but is considered a separate holiday on the Hebrew calendar. *Sukkot*, according to Leviticus 23:34, is celebrated for seven days, but only on the first and eighth days is labor forbidden. In the diaspora, *Shemini 'Atseret* is celebrated as a holiday on its own. The *sukkah** is no longer used; neither are the *lulav** and *etrog**. No particular symbols are associated with this day, which is seen as a continuation of the joy of *Sukkot*. In Israel, *Shemini 'Atseret* and *Simḥat Torah** are celebrated on the same day, and it takes on primarily the character of the latter.

The *Midrash** offers several explanations for the "extra" holiday. Pilgrims would have come a long way to Jerusalem in order to celebrate *Sukkot*, probably the most widely observed pilgrimage festival. Some came for nearly the whole month to dwell in the sacred city and to be in "God's courts." Loving their company as He does, God is like the king who asks his beloved guest to stay an extra day, for the pure enjoyment of being together. Other sources note that *Sukkot* is a universal holiday, when seventy bullocks are being offered over the course of the seven days in honor of the seventy nations of the world. God then invites Israel to stay an extra day just on their own, like the steward who stays in his master's court after all the great guests have departed.

As the last statutory day of the fall festival season, *Shemini 'Atseret* is the day when a prayer for rain is said in the *mussaf** prayer. This *geshem* prayer introduces the daily supplication for rain recited in each *'amidah** prayer through the rainy season, ending with *Pesaḥ**. Along with its parallel *tal* ("Dew"), recited on the first day of *Pesaḥ*, it is chanted in an awesome melody reminiscent of the *Rosh Hashanah** and *Yom Kippur** liturgy.

שמיטה/יובל

Shemitah/Yovel

SHEMITAH, the Sabbatical year, and *yovel*, the Jubilee, are part of ancient Biblical legislation that applies specifically to the Jewish people living in *Erets Yisrael**. These laws, recorded in Leviticus 25, remind Israel that the land belongs to God. We are only its stewards. Israel's role in the land is parallel to that of Adam in Eden, "to work it and guard it" (Genesis 2:15). The Land of Israel is a divine gift, dependent on the people's living up to the terms of its covenant.

"Guarding" the land means extending to it the rest that we are given in *Shabbat**. Before much was known about crop rotation and how it could reinvigorate the soil, the ancients sensed that farmland could be exhausted if overworked. The sabbatical year, requiring that the land be left fallow one year of each seven, is undoubtedly related to this awareness. During that *shemitah* year, there is to be neither planting nor harvest. Various other agricultural activities are also forbidden or severely limited. Thus the effects of the *shemitah* are actually spread over two years or more.

At the end of seven *shemitah* cycles, a jubilee is held. In this year, again one of rest for the soil, all rural land that had been sold or otherwise transferred from one owner to another was to be returned to its original family or tribal ownership. All loans within the community of Israel were to be forgiven. All Hebrew servants, having reached that status through indenture, were to be set free.

The *tanakh** records the *shemitah* and *yovel* legislation only in this hypothetical form. There is no story of the *shemitah* actually being observed in Biblical times or how people managed with it. The *Mishnah** and the Jerusalem *Talmud** do contain quite a bit more detail of the laws, which clearly were observed by farmers loyal to the rabbinic leadership in the first few centuries of the Common Era. After that, the *shemitah* and *yovel* were treated for hundreds of years as unpracticed parts of *halakhah**, parallel to Temple and priesthood laws that no longer had any practical application. The small Jewish communities of *Erets Yisrael* did not engage in agriculture, so there was no one to whom the rules applied.

With the beginning of an agriculture-based return to the land in the late 19th century, various ways were sought to get around the difficult demands of *shemitah* legislation, which placed nearly impossible burdens on struggling farm communities. Some pious Jews in Israel insist on eating only produce grown by non-Jewish farmers during the *shemitah* and the year following it. Others have come to accept the notion of a fictional "sale" of farmlands to non-Jewish owners during the Sabbatical. But unfortunately, rather little creative thought has been devoted to the implications of *shemitah* and *yovel* and how they might be applied in our day. Can a people who were taught to let the land rest now pollute that same land with chemical fertilizers that will ultimately destroy its natural richness? Are Jewish owners of land (or investors in companies that own land) and natural resources *anywhere* in the world allowed to strip them away at the consumers' will? Or is there a divine imperative, somehow emerging from these old restrictions on the use of land, to do so only with care and responsibility? The articulation of such responsibility, in convincing frameworks of both *aggadah** and *halakhah*, is an urgent need for contemporary Judaism.

שמחת תורה
Simhat Torah

SIMHAT TORAH (literally: "the joy of Torah") is the concluding day of the fall festival cycle. In the diaspora, it is the day after *Shemini 'Atseret** or the 24th day of the month *Tishrey.* In Israel, it is celebrated on the same day as *Shemini 'Atseret.*

The celebration of *Simhat Torah* began as a custom (*minhag**) of the Western European Jewish communities in the Middle Ages and spread throughout the Jewish world. On this day, the annual cycle of *Torah** reading is concluded and begins again, showing the constancy of Torah and its place in the life of the Jewish people. The final passage of Deuteronomy, the account of Moses' blessing and his death, is read by someone who is called *hatan Torah,* which means "bridegroom of Torah." Then, from a second scroll, the opening chapter of Genesis is read by a *hatan bereshit,* a "bridegroom of 'In the beginning.'" All this is done amid great merriment. On the eve of *Simhat Torah,* in preparation for this event, the Torah scrolls are taken out for dancing and celebration. The atmosphere in many synagogues is similar to that of *Purim*,* though there is a definite difference between the two events.

Structurally, *Simhat Torah* is parallel in the fall holidays to *Shavu'ot* in the cycle of the spring. It is the concluding day of the holy period on which Torah is given. *Simhat Torah* too may be seen as a time when Torah is received, imbibed, and taken into the self. Each of these concluding days sends Israel forth into the profane days ahead, but fortified with the Torah it will need to uplift and transform them.

סוכות

Sukkot

Sukkot, the festival of the fall full moon, is celebrated for seven days that begin on the 15th of *Tishrey.* This is the Biblical "seventh month," as prescribed in Leviticus 23:33 and Deuteronomy 16:13. *Sukkot* is a harvest festival, "the season of ingathering." As we gather the produce of the field into our homes for the winter, so does God gather us into God's special place, the *sukkah**.

Perhaps the original kernel of this festival lies in the transition our ancient ancestors made from nomadic to settled agriculture-based existence. The farmers kept in their hearts the ancient memory of life as wanderers. Once a year, at the time of the first fall full moon, they would go out and live in wanderers' tents for a week, just as at the spring full moon they took a week when they would eat only nomads' bread, during the Festival of *Matzot (Matzah***)* that was to be joined to our *Pesaḥ**. The *sukkah* came to be associated with harvest time, and later still with the huts in which the people of Israel lived during our forty years of wandering in the wilderness.

Sukkot is called "the season of our joy," and is meant to be the most joyous of all the festivals. This is not the frolicking joy of *Purim**, but a happiness born of deep satiety at the harvest and gratitude for God's gifts. We also rejoice that the season of judgment has passed, confident that our sins are forgiven and the way is clear for us to start life anew. Sheltered in God's love in the *sukkah,* we rejoice and dance before God with *lulav** and *etrog** in our hands. On the intermediate days of *Sukkot* a special libation ceremony occurred in the ancient Temple. The earliest rabbis, who still recalled the ceremony from the days before the Temple's destruction, said: "Whoever has not seen the joy of the Temple water-drawing has never seen joy at all!"

תשעה באב
Tish'ah be-Av

The ninth day of the month *Av*, or *Tish'ah be-Av*, is the classic day of mourning on the Hebrew calendar. Tradition has it that the First and Second Temples both were destroyed on that day. Various other calamities of Jewish history, including the edict of the expulsion of the Jews from Spain in 1492, are also associated with that date.

Tish'ah be-Av is (along with *Yom Kippur**) a full twenty-five-hour fast day, running from dusk until nightfall. Along with eating and drinking, it is forbidden to bathe or perfume oneself, to wear (leather) shoes, or to engage in sexual relations.

The synagogue is often darkened on the eve of *Tish'ah be-Av*. By the light of candles or other dim light, the community, as mourners, sit on low benches or on the floor, like mourners (*shiv'ah**), and chant the scroll of Lamentations. This is followed by the reading of *kinot*, mourning dirges bewailing the destruction of Jerusalem as well as the persecution of Jews, composed mostly in the Middle Ages. The following morning service is characterized by further dirges, but also by the fact that *tefillin** are not worn, a sign of extreme distress. The *tefillin* are in fact worn during the afternoon (*minḥah**) service, so as not to neglect the daily obligation.

The establishment of a Jewish state and the conquest of old Jerusalem in 1967 have called into question the appropriateness of *Tish'ah be-Av* mourning in our day. In some national-religious circles, it was proposed to end the fast after an early *minḥah* service, turning the other half day over to rejoicing at the return to Zion. (In recent years, this attempt has fallen victim to the general tendency toward greater stringency within Orthodoxy.) Certainly the text of the *kinot*, and even of Lamentations itself, is hardly appropriate to the contemporary Jewish/Israeli situation. On the other hand, the abolition or curtailing of *Tish'ah be-Av* seems to make a messianic (*mashiah**) claim that is especially dangerous in our age. The return to Zion is a great historical event of our times. It has about it a ring of fulfillment of prophecy that cannot be denied. But that does not mean that we should be prepared to proclaim messiah. The ongoing presence of *Tish'ah be-Av* in our calendar, especially if we can shift the focus of its mourning from national destruction to moral failure, is a good reminder that redemption has not yet come, not even to Zion.

יום כיפור

Yom Kippur

YOM KIPPUR, the 10th day of *Tishrey*, is the holiest and most awesome day on the Hebrew calendar. It is called a "Sabbath of Sabbaths"; all work that is forbidden on the Sabbath is forbidden on *Yom Kippur* as well. In addition, it is a full fast day, which means that there are five special prohibitions: against eating and drinking, sexual relations, bathing, wearing (leather) shoes, and wearing perfumes. The Talmudic (*Talmud**) tractate dealing with *Yom Kippur* is simply called "The Day."

Yom Kippur is also one of the most ancient Jewish festivals. Its ritual, probably as practiced in First Temple times, is fully elaborated in Leviticus 16. The purpose of that ritual was to atone for Israel, its priests, and its Temple, to "cover" their sins and allow for a new purity. This was accomplished by sacrifice, the sprinkling of blood, and the unique expulsion of the scapegoat, who carried the sins of Israel off into the wilderness.

An account of that Temple rite, called the *'avodah*, is still read in the traditional synagogue during the *Yom Kippur mussaf** service. But *Yom Kippur* has been transformed in the rabbinic tradition to a day of intense prayer and soul-searching, encouraged by the atmosphere of the fast. There are five prayer services on *Yom Kippur*: *'arvit** on the eve of the holy day (preceded by *Kol Nidre**), *shaharit,* mussaf,* and *minhah** of the day, and a special concluding service called *ne'ilah**. To each of these, a special penitential section called *selihot* is added; in the first four services, this also includes a lengthy confession of sins. The penitential hymns or *selihot* are interspersed with frequent calling out of God's thirteen attributes, which are found in Exodus 34:6–7. This is the formula Moses mysteriously heard recited in the moment when God forgave Israel the sin of the golden calf, and it is still felt to have great power to arouse the forgiveness of sin.

Many of the great liturgical compositions of the synagogue, both poetic and musical, have been written for *Yom Kippur*. It is generally considered to be a full day of prayer. In traditional synagogues, there may be just a brief break between the *mussaf* and *minḥah* services. The leaders of prayer and many others are dressed in white, symbolizing innocence, and the *aron kodesh** and *Torah** scrolls are also covered in white, as they are throughout the penitential season. The length and repetitious quality of the prayer services on *Yom Kippur* have a cathartic effect, and by the end of the fast, following the appearance of three stars in the evening sky, we are filled with a sense of both exhaustion and cleansing.

The *Mishnah** makes it clear that the purification of *Yom Kippur* is effective only for transgressions against God. Sins against our fellow person require that person's forgiveness. Since Jews do not want to go through *Yom Kippur* with the burden of sin still upon them, it is customary before or on *Yom Kippur* for us to ask forgiveness of one another.

יוֹם טוֹב

Yom Tov

THIS USUAL Hebrew term for "festival" simply means "good day."
In fact, the Yiddish holiday greeting "*gut yontiff* (*yom tov*)" is really
a redundancy: "Have a good good-day!"

The term is applied to all holidays when work is forbidden. (How
good a day can it be if you have to go to work?). Technically, therefore, *Yom Kippur** is a *yom tov,* and "*gut yontiff*" (or even the modern Hebrew equivalent, "*hag sameah*" or "happy holiday") may be
used as a greeting. *Purim** and *Hanukkah**, however, are not *yom
tov,* since work is permitted on them. Each of these has its own separate greeting. (In Yiddish these are: "*a freylekhn hanuke*" and "*gut
purim,*" and in Hebrew they are *hag orim sameah* and *Purim
sameah.*)

The chief element in the celebration of *yom tov* is joy (unlike
*Shabbat**, when rest takes precedence). The *Talmud** says that
such joy should include drinking wine and eating meat (vegetarians may fulfill the obligation in other ways, such as eating a little
more eggplant). Because food is central to any Jewish concept of
joyous celebration, the strict Sabbath rules against cooking are
relaxed on *yom tov.* We may kindle, use, and transfer fire. Since
these are permitted for *yom tov* cooking, these leniencies are
allowed for other purposes as well. We may not, however, use *yom
tov* to prepare food for the future, unless *Shabbat* is immediately
approaching.

Singing is another expression of joy in which Jews typically
engage on *yom tov.* Both in the synagogue (especially at *hallel**)
and at the holiday table at home, song is a part of *yom tov*
celebration, the joy of which is supposed to be "half for God, half
for yourselves."

יארצייט

Yortseit

Yortseit (literally, in Yiddish, "year's time") is the anniversary of a death. It is traditional to commemorate the *yortseit* of parents, spouses, siblings, and children.

Yortseit is observed on the actual date of death (not burial) according to the Hebrew calendar. Its observance is not postponed by *Shabbat** or *yom tov**. *Kaddish** is recited in the synagogue. A person who is observing a *yortseit* and is capable of leading a (weekday) service will be asked to do so. If the *Torah** is read that day, it is possible to ask that a memorial prayer be recited following the Torah reading, although that is usually done only for a first *yortseit* or in memory of an important rabbi or community leader. It is also customary to give to charity on a *yortseit*. In some places, the person observing *yortseit* brings food and drink to be served following the *shaharit** service.

A memorial candle is lighted at home. If the *yortseit* falls on a Sabbath or festival, care is taken to light the *yortseit* candle before lighting the *Shabbat* or *yom tov* candles. Visits to the cemetery are also conducted on or near the *yortseit*.

Index of English Terms

About JEWISH LIGHTS Publishing

People of all faiths and backgrounds yearn for books that attract, engage, educate and spiritually inspire.

Our principal goal is to stimulate thought and help all people learn about who the Jewish People are, where they come from, and what the future can be made to hold. While people of our diverse Jewish heritage are the primary audience, our books speak to people in the Christian world as well and will broaden their understanding of Judaism and the roots of their own faith.

We bring to you authors who are at the forefront of spiritual thought and experience. While each has something different to say, they all say it in a voice that you can hear.

Our books are designed to welcome you and then to engage, stimulate and inspire. We judge our success not only by whether or not our books are beautiful and commercially successful, but by whether or not they make a difference in your life.

We at Jewish Lights take great care to produce beautiful books that present meaningful spiritual content in a form that reflects the art of making high quality books. Therefore, we want to acknowledge those who contributed to the production of this book.

PRODUCTION
Bridgett Taylor

EDITORIAL & PROOFREADING
Sandra Korinchak & Martha McKinney

TEXT DESIGN
The Philidor Company, Cambridge, MA

PRINTING AND BINDING
Lake Book, Melrose Park, Illinois

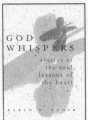

Spirituality

HOW TO BE A PERFECT STRANGER, In 2 Volumes
A Guide to Etiquette in Other People's Religious Ceremonies
Edited by *Stuart M. Matlins & Arthur J. Magida*

"A book that belongs in every living room, library and office!"

Explains the rituals and celebrations of America's major religions/denominations, helping an interested guest to feel comfortable, participate to the fullest extent possible, and avoid violating anyone's religious principles.

•Award Winner•

Answers practical questions from the perspective of *any* other faith.

VOL. 1: America's Largest Faiths

VOL. 1 COVERS: Assemblies of God • Baptist • Buddhist • Christian Science • Churches of Christ • Disciples of Christ • Episcopalian • Greek Orthodox • Hindu • Islam • Jehovah's Witnesses • Jewish • Lutheran • Methodist • Mormon • Presbyterian • Quaker • Roman Catholic • Seventh-day Adventist • United Church of Christ

6" x 9", 432 pp. Hardcover, ISBN 1-879045-39-7 **$24.95**

VOL. 2: Other Faiths in America

VOL. 2 COVERS: African American Methodist Churches • Baha'i • Christian and Missionary Alliance • Christian Congregation • Church of the Brethren • Church of the Nazarene • Evangelical Free Church of America • International Church of the Foursquare Gospel • International Pentecostal Holiness Church • Mennonite/Amish • Native American • Orthodox Churches • Pentecostal Church of God • Reformed Church of America • Sikh • Unitarian Universalist • Wesleyan

6" x 9", 416 pp. HC, ISBN 1-879045-63-X **$24.95**

GOD & THE BIG BANG
Discovering Harmony Between Science & Spirituality
by *Daniel C. Matt*

Mysticism and science: What do they have in common? How can one enlighten the other? By drawing on modern cosmology and ancient Kabbalah, Matt shows how science and religion can together enrich our spiritual awareness and help us recover a sense of wonder and find our place in the universe.

"This poetic new book...helps us to understand the human meaning of creation."
—*Joel Primack, leading cosmologist, Professor of Physics, University of California, Santa Cruz*

•Award Winner•

6" x 9", 216 pp. Quality Paperback, ISBN 1-879045-89-3 **$16.95**; HC, ISBN-48-6 **$21.95**

MINDING THE TEMPLE OF THE SOUL
Balancing Body, Mind, & Spirit through Traditional Jewish Prayer, Movement, & Meditation
by *Tamar Frankiel* and *Judy Greenfeld*

This new spiritual approach to physical health introduces readers to a spiritual tradition that affirms the body and enables them to reconceive their bodies in a more positive light. Relying on Kabbalistic teachings and other Jewish traditions, it shows us how to be more responsible for our own psychological and physical health. Focuses on the discipline of prayer, simple Tai Chi–like exercises and body positions, and guides the reader throughout, step-by-step, with diagrams, sketches and meditations.

7" x 10", 184 pp. Quality Paperback Original, illus., ISBN 1-879045-64-8 **$16.95**

Audiotape of the Blessings, Movements & Meditations (60-min. cassette) **$9.95**
Videotape of the Movements & Meditations (46-min. VHS) **$20.00**

Spirituality

MEDITATION FROM THE HEART OF JUDAISM
Today's Teachers Share Their Practices, Techniques, and Faith
Edited by *Avram Davis*

A "how-to" guide for both beginning and experienced meditators, it will help you start meditating or help you enhance your practice.

Twenty-two masters of meditation explain why and how they meditate. *A detailed compendium of the experts' "Best Practices"* offers practical advice and starting points.

6" x 9", 256 pp. Quality Paperback, ISBN 1-58023-049-0 **$16.95**; HC,

HC ISBBN 1-879045-77-X **$21.95**

SELF, STRUGGLE & CHANGE
Family Conflict Stories in Genesis and Their Healing Insights for Our Lives
by *Norman J. Cohen*

How do I find greater wholeness in my life and in my family's life?

The people described by the biblical writers of Genesis were in situations and relationships very much like our own. We identify with them. Their stories still speak to us because they are about the same problems we deal with every day. Here a modern master of biblical interpretation brings us greater understanding of the ancient text and of ourselves in this intriguing re-telling of conflict between husband and wife, father and son, brothers, and sisters.

6" x 9", 224 pp. Quality Paperback, ISBN 1-879045-66-4 **$16.95**; HC, ISBN-19-2 **$21.95**

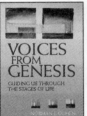

VOICES FROM GENESIS
Guiding Us Through the Stages of Life
by *Norman J. Cohen*

A brilliant blending of modern midrash and the life stages of Erik Erikson's developmental psychology. Shows how the pathways of our lives are quite similar to those of the leading figures of Genesis who speak directly to us, telling of their spiritual and emotional journeys.

6" x 9", 192 pp. HC, ISBN 1-879045-75-3 **$21.95**

ISRAEL—A SPIRITUAL TRAVEL GUIDE
A Companion for the Modern Jewish Pilgrim
by *Rabbi Lawrence A. Hoffman*

Be spiritually prepared for your journey to Israel.

A Jewish spiritual travel guide to Israel, helping today's pilgrim tap into the deep spiritual meaning of the ancient—and modern—sites of the Holy Land. Combines in quick reference format ancient blessings, medieval prayers, biblical and historical references, and modern poetry. The only guidebook that helps readers to prepare spiritually for the occasion. More than a guide book: It is a spiritual map.

4¾" x 10", 256 pp. Quality Paperback Original, ISBN 1-879045-56-7 **$18.95**   •AWARD WINNER•

Spirituality—The Kushner Series

EYES REMADE FOR WONDER
A Lawrence Kushner Reader
Introduction by *Thomas Moore*

A treasury of insight from one of the most creative spiritual thinkers in America. Whether you are new to Kushner or a devoted fan, this is the place to begin. With samplings from each of Kushner's works, and a generous amount of new material, this is a book to be savored, to be read and reread, each time discovering deeper layers of meaning in our lives. Offers something unique to both the spiritual seeker and the committed person of faith.

6" x 9", 240 pp. Quality PB, ISBN 1-58023-042-3 **$16.95**; HC, ISBN -014-8 **$23.95**

•AWARD WINNER•

INVISIBLE LINES OF CONNECTION
Sacred Stories of the Ordinary
by *Lawrence Kushner*

Through his everyday encounters with family, friends, colleagues and strangers, Kushner takes us deeply into our lives, finding flashes of spiritual insight in the process.

5½" x 8½", 160 pp. Quality Paperback, ISBN 1-879045-98-2 **$15.95**

HC, ISBN -52-4 **$21.95**

HONEY FROM THE ROCK
An Easy Introduction to Jewish Mysticism

by *Lawrence Kushner*

"Quite simply the easiest introduction to Jewish mysticism you can read."

An introduction to the ten gates of Jewish mysticism and how it applies to daily life.

6" x 9", 168 pp. Quality Paperback, ISBN 1-879045-02-8 **$14.95**

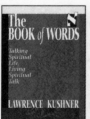

THE BOOK OF WORDS
Talking Spiritual Life, Living Spiritual Talk
by *Lawrence Kushner*

In the incomparable manner of his extraordinary *The Book of Letters*, Kushner now lifts up and shakes the dust off primary religious words we use to describe the spiritual dimension of life. For each word Kushner offers us a startling, moving and insightful explication. He concludes with a short exercise that helps unite the spirit of the word with our actions in the world.

6" x 9", 152 pp. 2-color text, Quality PB ISBN 1-58023-020-2 **$16.95**; HC, ISBN 1-879045-35-4 **$21.95**

THE BOOK OF LETTERS
A Mystical Hebrew Alphabet
by *Rabbi Lawrence Kushner*

In calligraphy by the author. Folktales about and exploration of the mystical meanings of the Hebrew Alphabet. Draws from ancient Judaic sources, weaving Talmudic commentary, Hasidic folktales, and kabbalistic mysteries around the letters.

• **Popular Hardcover Edition** 6" x 9", 80 pp. HC, two colors, inspiring new Foreword. ISBN 1-879045-00-1 **$24.95**

• **Deluxe Gift Edition** 9" x 12", 80 pp. HC, four-color text, ornamentation, in a beautiful slipcase. **$79.95**

•AWARD WINNER•

• **Collector's Limited Edition** 9" x 12", 80 pp. HC, gold-embossed pages, hand-assembled slipcase. With silkscreened print. **Limited to 500 signed and numbered copies.** ISBN 1-879045-04-4 **$349.00**

Spirituality

GOD WAS IN THIS PLACE & I, i DID NOT KNOW
Finding Self, Spirituality & Ultimate Meaning
by *Lawrence Kushner*

Who am I? Who is God? Kushner creates inspiring interpretations of Jacob's dream in Genesis, opening a window into Jewish spirituality for people of all faiths and backgrounds.

6" x 9", 192 pp. Quality Paperback, ISBN 1-879045-33-8 **$16.95**

THE RIVER OF LIGHT
Spirituality, Judaism, Consciousness
by *Lawrence Kushner*

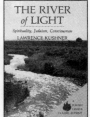

A "manual" for all spiritual travelers who would attempt a spiritual journey in our times. Taking us step by step, Kushner allows us to discover the meaning of our own quest: "to allow the river of light—the deepest currents of consciousness—to rise to the surface and animate our lives."

6" x 9", 180 pp. Quality Paperback, ISBN 1-879045-03-6 **$14.95**

GODWRESTLING—ROUND 2
Ancient Wisdom, Future Paths
by *Arthur Waskow*

This 20th-anniversary sequel to a seminal book of the Jewish renewal movement deals with spirituality in relation to personal growth, marriage, ecology, feminism, politics, and more.

6" x 9", 352 pp. Quality Paperback, ISBN 1-879045-72-9 **$18.95**

HC, ISBN -45-1 **$23.95**

•AWARD WINNER•

ECOLOGY & THE JEWISH SPIRIT
Where Nature & the Sacred Meet
Edited and with Introductions by *Ellen Bernstein*

What is nature's place in our spiritual lives?

A focus on nature is part of the fabric of Jewish thought. Here, experts bring us a richer understanding of the long-neglected themes of nature that are woven through the biblical creation story, ancient texts, traditional law, the holiday cycles, prayer, *mitzvot* (good deeds), and community.

6" x 9", 288 pp. HC, ISBN 1-879045-88-5 **$23.95**

BEING GOD'S PARTNER
How to Find the Hidden Link Between
Spirituality and Your Work
by *Jeffrey K. Salkin*; Introduction by *Norman Lear*

Will challenge people of every denomination to reconcile the cares of work and soul. A groundbreaking book about spirituality and the work world, from a Jewish perspective. Offers practical suggestions for balancing your professional life and spiritual self.

6" x 9", 192 pp. Quality Paperback, ISBN 1-879045-65-6 **$16.95**

HC, ISBN -37-0 **$19.95**

Spirituality

MY PEOPLE'S PRAYER BOOK
Traditional Prayers, Modern Commentaries
Vol. 1—The *Sh'ma* and Its Blessings
Vol. 2—The *Amidah*
Vol. 3—*P'sukei D'zimrah* (Morning Psalms)
Edited by *Rabbi Lawrence A. Hoffman*

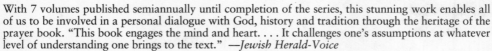

Provides a diverse and exciting commentary to the traditional liturgy, written by 10 of today's most respected scholars and teachers from all perspectives of the Jewish world.

With 7 volumes published semiannually until completion of the series, this stunning work enables all of us to be involved in a personal dialogue with God, history and tradition through the heritage of the prayer book. "This book engages the mind and heart. . . . It challenges one's assumptions at whatever level of understanding one brings to the text." —*Jewish Herald-Voice*

Vol. 1: 7" x 10", 168 pp. HC, ISBN 1-879045-79-6 **$21.95**
Vol. 2: 7" x 10", 240 pp. HC, ISBN 1-879045-80-X **$21.95**
Vol. 3: 7" x 10", 192 pp. (est.) HC, ISBN 1-879045-81-8 **$21.95**

FINDING JOY
A Practical Spiritual Guide to Happiness
by *Dannel I. Schwartz* with *Mark Hass*

Searching for happiness in our modern world of stress and struggle is common; *finding* it is more unusual. This guide explores and explains how to find joy through a time-honored, creative—and surprisingly practical—approach based on the teachings of Jewish mysticism and Kabbalah.

"Lovely, simple introduction to Kabbalah....a singular contribution...."
—*American Library Association's* Booklist

•AWARD WINNER•
6" x 9", 192 pp. Quality PB, ISBN 1-58023-009-1 **$14.95** HC, ISBN 1-879045-53-2 **$19.95**

THE DEATH OF DEATH
Resurrection and Immortality in Jewish Thought
by *Neil Gillman*

Explores the original and compelling argument that Judaism, a religion often thought to pay little attention to the afterlife, not only offers us rich ideas on the subject—but delivers a deathblow to death itself.

6" x 9", 336 pp., HC, ISBN 1-879045-61-3 **$23.95**

THE EMPTY CHAIR: FINDING HOPE & JOY
Timeless Wisdom from a Hasidic Master,
Rebbe Nachman of Breslov
Adapted by *Moshe Mykoff* and the *Breslov Research Institute*

A "little treasure" of aphorisms and advice for living joyously and spiritually today, written 200 years ago, but startlingly fresh in meaning and use.
Teacher, guide and spiritual master—Rebbe Nachman provides vital words of inspiration and wisdom for life today for people of any faith, or of no faith.

•AWARD WINNER• "For anyone of any faith, this is a book of healing and wholeness, of being alive!"
— *Bookviews*

4" x 6", 128 pp., 2-color text, Deluxe Paperback, ISBN 1-879045-67-2 **$9.95**

THE GENTLE WEAPON
Prayers for Everyday and Not-So-Everyday Moments
Adapted by *Moshe Mykoff* and *S.C. Mizrahi*,
together with the *Breslov Research Institute*

A small treasury of prayers for people of all faiths, based on the Jewish wisdom tradition. The perfect companion to *The Empty Chair: Finding Hope and Joy*, and to our stressful lives.

4" x 6", 144 pp., 2-color text, Deluxe Paperback, ISBN 1-58023-022-9 **$9.95**

Healing/Recovery/Wellness

Experts Praise *Twelve Jewish Steps to Recovery*

"Recommended reading for people of all denominations."
—*Rabbi Abraham J. Twerski, M.D.*

TWELVE JEWISH STEPS TO RECOVERY
A Personal Guide to Turning from Alcoholism & Other Addictions...Drugs, Food, Gambling, Sex...
by *Rabbi Kerry M. Olitzky & Stuart A. Copans, M.D.*
Preface by *Abraham J. Twerski, M.D.*; Intro. by *Rabbi Sheldon Zimmerman*; "Getting Help" by *JACS Foundation*

A Jewish perspective on the Twelve Steps of addiction recovery programs with consolation, inspiration and motivation for recovery. It draws from traditional sources and quotes from what recovering Jewish people say about their experiences with addictions of all kinds. Inspiring illustrations of the twelve gates of the Old City of Jerusalem introduce each step.

6" x 9", 136 pp. Quality Paperback, ISBN 1-879045-09-5 **$13.95**

Recovery from Codependence: A Jewish Twelve Steps Guide to Healing Your Soul
by Rabbi Kerry M. Olitzky
6" x 9", 160 pp. Quality Paperback Original, ISBN 1-879045-32-X **$13.95**; HC, ISBN -27-3 **$21.95**

Renewed Each Day: Daily Twelve Step Recovery Meditations Based on the Bible
by Rabbi Kerry M. Olitzky & Aaron Z.
6" x 9", Quality Paperback Original, **V. I**, 224 pp. **$14.95 V. II**, 280 pp. **$16.95**

One Hundred Blessings Every Day: Daily Twelve Step Recovery Affirmations, Exercises for Personal Growth & Renewal Reflecting Seasons of the Jewish Year
by Rabbi Kerry M. Olitzky
4½" x 6½", 432 pp. Quality Paperback Original, ISBN 1-879045-30-3 **$14.95**

HEALING OF SOUL, HEALING OF BODY
Spiritual Leaders Unfold the Strength and Solace in Psalms
Edited by *Rabbi Simkha Y. Weintraub, CSW, for The Jewish Healing Center*

A source of solace for those who are facing illness, as well as those who care for them. The ten Psalms which form the core of this healing resource were originally selected 200 years ago by Rabbi Nachman of Breslov as a "complete remedy." Today, for anyone coping with illness, they continue to provide a wellspring of strength. Each Psalm is newly translated, making it clear and accessible, and each one is introduced by an eminent rabbi, men and women reflecting different movements and backgrounds. To all who are living with the pain and uncertainty of illness, this spiritual resource offers an anchor of spiritual comfort.

"Will bring comfort to anyone fortunate enough to read it. This gentle book is a luminous gem of wisdom."
—*Larry Dossey, M.D., author of* Healing Words: The Power of Prayer & the Practice of Medicine

6" x 9", 128 pp. Quality Paperback Original, illus., 2-color text, ISBN 1-879045-31-1 **$14.95**

Theology/Philosophy

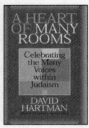

A HEART OF MANY ROOMS
Celebrating the Many Voices within Judaism
by *David Hartman*

With clarity, passion and outstanding scholarship, David Hartman addresses the spiritual and theological questions that face all Jews and all people today. From the perspective of traditional Judaism, he helps us understand the varieties of 20th-century Jewish practice and shows that commitment to both Jewish tradition and to pluralism can create bridges of understanding between people of different religious convictions.

"An extraordinary book, devoid of stereotypic thinking; lucid and pertinent, a modern classic."
—*Michael Walzer, Institute for Advanced Study, Princeton*

6" x 9", 352 pp. HC, ISBN 1-58023-048-2 **$24.95**

*WINNER,
National Jewish
Book Award*

A LIVING COVENANT
The Innovative Spirit in Traditional Judaism
by *David Hartman*

The Judaic tradition is often seen as being more concerned with uncritical obedience to law than with individual freedom and responsibility. Hartman challenges this approach by revealing a Judaism grounded in a covenant—a relational framework—informed by the metaphor of marital love rather than that of parent-child dependency.

"Jews and non-Jews, liberals and traditionalists will see classic Judaism anew in these pages." —*Dr. Eugene B. Borowitz,*
Hebrew Union College–Jewish Institute of Religion

•AWARD WINNER•

6" x 9", 368 pp. Quality Paperback, ISBN 1-58023-011-3 **$18.95**

• CLASSICS BY ABRAHAM JOSHUA HESCHEL •

The Earth Is the Lord's: The Inner World of the Jew in Eastern Europe
5½" x 8", 112 pp, Quality Paperback, ISBN 1-879045-42-7 **$13.95**

Israel: An Echo of Eternity with new Introduction by Susannah Heschel
5½" x 8", 272 pp, Quality Paperback, ISBN 1-879045-70-2 **$18.95**

A Passion for Truth: Despair and Hope in Hasidism
5½" x 8", 352 pp, Quality Paperback, ISBN 1-879045-41-9 **$18.95**

• THEOLOGY & PHILOSOPHY...Other books•

Aspects of Rabbinic Theology by Solomon Schechter, with a new Introduction by Neil Gillman 6" x 9", 440 pp, Quality Paperback, ISBN 1-879045-24-9 **$18.95**

The Last Trial: On the Legends and Lore of the Command to Abraham to Offer Isaac as a Sacrifice by Shalom Spiegel, with a new Introduction by Judah Goldin
6" x 9", 208 pp, Quality Paperback, ISBN 1-879045-29-X **$17.95**

Judaism and Modern Man: An Interpretation of Jewish Religion by Will Herberg; new Introduction by Neil Gillman 5½" x 8½", 336 pp, Quality Paperback, ISBN 1-879045-87-7 **$18.95**

Seeking the Path to Life: Theological Meditations On God and the Nature of People, Love, Life and Death by Rabbi Ira F. Stone
6" x 9", 132 pp, Quality Paperback, ISBN 1-879045-47-8 **$14.95**; HC, ISBN 1-879045-17-6 **$19.95**

The Spirit of Renewal: Finding Faith After the Holocaust by Edward Feld
6" x 9", 224 pp, Quality Paperback, ISBN 1-879045-40-0 **$16.95**

Tormented Master: The Life and Spiritual Quest of Rabbi Nahman of Bratslav by Arthur Green 6" x 9", 408 pp, Quality Paperback, ISBN 1-879045-11-7 **$18.95**

Your Word Is Fire Ed. and trans. with a new Introduction by Arthur Green and Barry W. Holtz 6" x 9", 152 pp, Quality Paperback, ISBN 1-879045-25-7 **$14.95**

Life Cycle

GRIEF IN OUR SEASONS
A Mourner's Kaddish Companion
by *Rabbi Kerry M. Olitzky*

Strength from the Jewish tradition for the first year of mourning.

Provides a wise and inspiring selection of sacred Jewish writings and a simple, powerful ancient ritual for mourners to read each day, to help hold the memory of their loved ones in their hearts. It offers a comforting, step-by-step daily link to saying *Kaddish*.

"A hopeful, compassionate guide along the journey from grief to rebirth from mourning to a new morning."
—*Rabbi Levi Meier, Ph.D., Chaplain, Cedars–Sinai Medical Center, Los Angeles*

4½" x 6½", 448 pp. Quality Paperback Original, ISBN 1-879045-55-9 **$15.95**

MOURNING & MITZVAH
• WITH OVER 60 GUIDED EXERCISES •
A Guided Journal for Walking the Mourner's Path Through Grief to Healing
by *Anne Brener, L.C.S.W.;*
Foreword by *Rabbi Jack Riemer;* Introduction by *Rabbi William Cutter*

"Fully engaging in mourning means you will be a different person than before you began." **For those who mourn a death, for those who would help them,** for those who face a loss of any kind, Brener teaches us the power and strength available to us in the fully experienced mourning process. Guided writing exercises help stimulate the processes of both conscious and unconscious healing.

"A stunning book! It offers an exploration in depth of the place where psychology and religious ritual intersect, and the name of that place is Truth."
—*Rabbi Harold Kushner, author of* When Bad Things Happen to Good People

7½" x 9", 288 pp. Quality Paperback Original, ISBN 1-879045-23-0 **$19.95**

A TIME TO MOURN, A TIME TO COMFORT
A Guide to Jewish Bereavement and Comfort
by *Dr. Ron Wolfson*

A guide to meeting the needs of those who mourn and those who seek to provide comfort in times of sadness. While this book is written from a layperson's point of view, it also includes the specifics for funeral preparations and practical guidance for preparing the home and family to sit *shiva*.

"A sensitive and perceptive guide to Jewish tradition. Both those who mourn and those who comfort will find it a map to accompany them through the whirlwind."

—*Deborah E. Lipstadt, Emory University*
7" x 9", 336 pp. Quality Paperback, ISBN 1-879045-96-6 **$16.95**

WHEN A GRANDPARENT DIES
A Kid's Own Remembering Workbook for Dealing with Shiva and the Year Beyond
by *Nechama Liss-Levinson, Ph.D.*

Drawing insights from both psychology and Jewish tradition, this workbook helps children participate in the process of mourning, offering guided exercises, rituals, and places to write, draw, list, create and express their feelings.

"Will bring support, guidance, and understanding for countless children, teachers, and health professionals."
—*Rabbi Earl A. Grollman, D.D., author of* Talking about Death

8" x 10", 48 pp. HC, illus., 2-color text, ISBN 1-879045-44-3 **$15.95**

Life Cycle

TEARS OF SORROW, SEEDS OF HOPE
A Jewish Spiritual Companion for Infertility and Pregnancy Loss
by *Rabbi Nina Beth Cardin*

Many people who endure the emotional suffering of infertility, pregnancy loss, or stillbirth bear this sorrow alone. Rarely is the experience of loss and infertility discussed with anyone but close friends and family members. Despite the private nature of the pain, many women and men would welcome the opportunity to be comforted by family and a community who would understand the pain and loneliness they feel, and the emptiness caused by the loss that is without a face, a name, or a grave.

Tears of Sorrow, Seeds of Hope is a spiritual companion that enables us to mourn infertility, a lost pregnancy, or a stillbirth within the prayers, rituals, and meditation of Judaism. By drawing deeply on the texts of tradition, it creates readings and rites of mourning, and through them provides a wellspring of compassion, solace—and hope.

6" x 9", 192 pp. HC, ISBN 1-58023-017-2 **$19.95**

•AWARD WINNER•

LIFECYCLES
V. 1: Jewish Women on Life Passages & Personal Milestones
Edited and with Introductions by *Rabbi Debra Orenstein*
V. 2: Jewish Women on Biblical Themes in Contemporary Life
Edited and with Introductions by
Rabbi Debra Orenstein and *Rabbi Jane Rachel Litman*

This unique multivolume collaboration brings together over one hundred women writers, rabbis, and scholars to create the first comprehensive work on Jewish life cycle that fully includes women's perspectives.

V. 1: 6" x 9", 480 pp. Quality Paperback, ISBN 1-58023-018-0 **$19.95**
HC, ISBN 1-879045-14-1 **$24.95**

V. 2: 6" x 9", 464 pp. Quality Paperback, ISBN 1-58023-019-9 **$19.95**
HC, ISBN 1-879045-15-X **$24.95**

LIFE CYCLE— The Art of Jewish Living Series for Holiday Observance
by Dr. Ron Wolfson

Hanukkah—7" x 9", 192 pp. Quality Paperback, ISBN 1-879045-97-4 **$16.95**

The Shabbat Seder—7" x 9", 272 pp. Quality Paperback, ISBN 1-879045-90-7 **$16.95**;
Booklet of Blessings **$5.00**; Audiocassette of Blessings **$6.00**; Teacher's Guide **$4.95**

The Passover Seder—7" x 9", 336 pp. Quality Paperback, ISBN 1-879045-93-1 **$16.95**;
Passover Workbook, **$6.95**; Audiocassette of Blessings, **$6.00**; Teacher's Guide, **$4.95**

• LIFE CYCLE...Other Books •

A Heart of Wisdom: Making the Jewish Journey from Midlife Through the Elder Years
Ed. by Susan Berrin 6" x 9", 384 pp. Quality Paperback, ISBN 1-58023-051-2, **$18.95**;
HC, ISBN 1-879045-73-7 **$24.95**

Bar/Bat Mitzvah Basics: A Practical Family Guide to Coming of Age Together
Ed. by Cantor Helen Leneman 6" x 9", 240 pp. Quality Paperback, ISBN 1-879045-54-0 **$16.95**

Embracing the Covenant: Converts to Judaism Talk About Why & How
Ed. and with Intros. by Rabbi Allan L. Berkowitz and Patti Moskovitz
6" x 9", 192 pp. Quality Paperback, ISBN 1-879045-50-8 **$15.95**

For Kids—Putting God on Your Guest List: How to Claim the Spiritual Meaning of Your Bar or Bat Mitzvah by Rabbi Jeffrey K. Salkin
6" x 9", 144 pp. Quality Paperback Original, ISBN 1-58023-015-6 **$14.95**

The New Jewish Baby Book: Names, Ceremonies, Customs—A Guide for Today's Families by Anita Diamant 6" x 9", 336 pp. Quality Paperback, ISBN 1-879045-28-1 **$16.95**

Putting God on the Guest List, 2nd Ed.: How to Reclaim the Spiritual Meaning of Your Child's Bar or Bat Mitzvah by Rabbi Jeffrey K. Salkin
6" x 9", 224 pp. Quality Paperback, ISBN 1-897045-59-1 **$16.95**; HC, ISBN 1-879045-58-3 **$24.95**

So That Your Values Live On: Ethical Wills & How to Prepare Them
Ed. by Rabbi Jack Riemer & Professor Nathaniel Stampfer
6" x 9", 272 pp. Quality Paperback, ISBN 1-879045-34-6 **$17.95**

Children's Spirituality

A PRAYER FOR THE EARTH
The Story of Naamah, Noah's Wife

For ages 4 and up

by *Sandy Eisenberg Sasso*
Full-color illustrations by *Bethanne Andersen*

NONDENOMINATIONAL, NONSECTARIAN

This new story, based on an ancient text, opens readers' religious imaginations to new ideas about the well-known story of the Flood. When God tells Noah to bring the animals of the world onto the ark, God *also* calls on Naamah, Noah's wife, to save each plant on Earth.

"A lovely tale....Children of all ages should be drawn to this parable for our times."
> —*Tomie dePaola, artist/author of books for children*

•AWARD WINNER•

9" x 12", 32 pp. HC, Full-color illus., ISBN 1-879045-60-5 **$16.95**

THE 11TH COMMANDMENT
Wisdom from Our Children

For all ages

by The Children of America

MULTICULTURAL, NONDENOMINATIONAL, NONSECTARIAN

"If there were an Eleventh Commandment, what would it be?"

Children of many religious denominations across America answer this question—in their own drawings and words—in *The 11th Commandment*.

"Wonderful....This unusual book provides both food for thought and insight into the hopes and fears of today's young."
> —*American Library Association's* Booklist

8" x 10", 48 pp. HC, Full-color illus., ISBN 1-879045-46-X **$16.95**

SHARING BLESSINGS
Children's Stories for Exploring the Spirit of the Jewish Holidays

For ages 6 and up

by *Rahel Musleah* and *Rabbi Michael Klayman*
Full-color illustrations by *Mary O'Keefe Young*

**What is the spiritual message of each of the Jewish holidays?
How do we teach it to our children?**

Many books tell children about the historical significance and customs of the holidays. Now, through engaging, creative stories about one family's spiritual preparation, *Sharing Blessings* explores ways to get into the *spirit* of 13 different holidays.

"A beguiling introduction to important Jewish values by way of the holidays."
> —*Rabbi Harold Kushner, author of* When Bad Things Happen to Good People *and* How Good Do We Have to Be?

7" x 10", 64 pp. HC, Full-color illus., ISBN 1-879045-71-0 **$18.95**

THE BOOK OF MIRACLES
A Young Person's Guide to Jewish Spiritual Awareness

For ages 9–13

by *Lawrence Kushner*

With a Special 10th Anniversary Introduction and all new illustrations by the author.

From the miracle at the Red Sea to the miracle of waking up this morning, this intriguing book introduces kids to a way of everyday spiritual thinking to last a lifetime. Kushner, whose award-winning books have brought spirituality to life for countless adults, now shows young people how to use Judaism as a foundation on which to build their lives.

6" x 9", 96 pp. HC, 2-color illus., ISBN 1-879045-78-8 **$16.95**

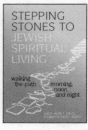

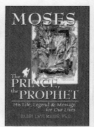